201 MORE Fat•Burning RECIPES

by

Cathi Graham

Front Cover:
Cavatappi Pasta with Fresh Tomato-Basil Sauce, page 125

201 MORE Fat-Burning Recipes
by
Cathi Graham

PUBLISHED BY
Publishing Solutions, a Division of PrintWest Communications Ltd.

SECOND PRINTING – MAY 2005

Library and Archives Canada Cataloguing in Publication

Graham, Cathi, 1956-
201 MORE fat-burning recipes / Cathi Graham

Includes index.
ISBN 1-897010-16-8

1. Reducing diets – Recipes. I. Title. II. Title: Two hundred and one more fat-burning recipes.

RM222.2.G735 2005   613.2'8   C2005-903021-6

Photography by: Patricia Holdsworth
Patricia Holdsworth Photography, Regina Saskatchewan

Printed and Produced in Canada by:
Centax Books, A Division of PrintWest Communications Ltd.
1150 Eighth Avenue, Regina, Saskatchewan, Canada S4R 1C9
(306) 525-2304   FAX (306) 757-2439
E-mail: centax@printwest.com   www.centaxbooks.com

HOW I LOST 186 POUNDS

Back in 1982 when I weighed over 326 pounds at 5'4", my feet and back hurt and my self-esteem was at an all-time low. I remember the pain and the shame and I remember going halfway up a short flight of stairs and feeling like my heart was pounding out of my chest. I remember being so fat I couldn't tie my shoelaces. I remember the embarrassment of going to a restaurant and getting glares from others as if I had no right to be there.

What they didn't know was that I had been on almost every diet known to mankind, from high-protein, to low-fat to the cabbage soup diet! The only thing I lost was the desire to go on another self-defeating diet!

The turning point came in 1982 when I went to the doctor's office and was diagnosed as "morbidly obese." That's when I knew I had to do something. I also knew I couldn't go on another hard-to-live-with diet. I started to research. I read; I researched university studies; went to Health Clinics and got information on Thermogenic Foods – foods that burn fat and flush fat out of the system. I researched on the correct combination of foods that would assimilate easily.

I discovered that soups stimulate CCK, a hormone that tells the brain you are full. How certain carbohydrates like barley and others would expand in your body to make you feel full longer. I found out how some proteins you snack on would keep you feeling fuller up to 40 minutes longer than others would. I also found out that not all fats are bad news. Essential fats, omega 3 and 6, assist metabolism and stabilize blood sugar – you have to eat essential fats to burn fat. What a Concept! Within 18 months I had lost 186 pounds. I have kept it off for over 20 years now!

All of this information worked for me. I knew in my heart of hearts that it would work for others. So I put all my energy and passion into developing the Fresh Start Metabolism Program™. It's like no other program out there. It offers 3 different programs to choose from – one diet does not fit all.

One plan is the Fast Start Plan, designed for quick results. The second plan is the Carbo Clean-Out Plan, designed for those who are carbo sensitive, love breads, pasta, sweets, etc. The third plan is the Glycemic Plan, which offers lots of flexibility and gives effective weight loss. It is great for those who want more starch choices and still want to be at their desired weight. What people like about the program is that it's flexible, yet gives you structure without counting calories or fat grams so you are not living in a "diet bubble."

Fresh Start has assisted thousands of men and women to live happy healthy lives. It gives a new set of tools to frustrated, diet-weary people, and a way to live life and lose weight. The Fresh Start Metabolism Program™ includes videos, audios, CDs, DVDs, meal plans, restaurant guides and an easy-to-use manual.

Over the years, the Fresh Start Metabolism Program™ has grown from a one-person program to a multi-faceted corporation. The basic premise has always remained the same – **To help people free themselves from the diet mentality forever and find happiness, health and peace of mind!**

To order the Fresh Start Metabolism Program™ call **1-800-66-FRESH** or go to our website at www.cathigraham.com

Get ready to Enjoy Your TRANSFORMATION!!

Cathi

201 MORE Fat•Burning RECIPES

TABLE OF CONTENTS

DEDICATION

Dedicated to my partner René
and my sister Mary B
whose love and support have always been there
to help me do what I love to do!

ACKNOWLEDGMENTS

I would like to thank the following people:

Morgan and Susanna Marshall for their loving, precise work in putting the cookbook into the computer and for their friendship which came as a result of our working together.

To Michael Price for the hours of proofreading and for his perceptive suggestions.

To Shop America, US and UK; TVSN – Australia; Danoz – Australia; TSC – Canada; and SLC Marketing for their expertise and marketing talent and for their belief in me and Fresh Start, in getting the Fresh Start Program out to hundreds of thousands of people, helping them live a healthier, more fulfilling lifestyle.

To my friend and mentor Rev. Hugh Cruickshank for his invaluable love which has taught me so much and supported me so generously.

Special thanks to my family, friends and wonderful secretary, Janet Walker, for their overwhelming support and for enthusiastically taste-testing my many recipes.

APPETIZERS

Chunky Artichoke Dip

Serve with vegetables or high-fiber crackers. To make tortilla or pita crisps for this or any other dip, cut tortilla or pita into wedges and put on a sprayed baking sheet. Brush lightly with oil and bake at 350°F for 5 to 10 minutes, or until lightly browned.

19 oz. can artichoke hearts, drained

¼ cup 5% ricotta cheese

¼ cup light sour cream OR 2% yogurt

¼ cup chopped fresh parsley

¼ cup chopped green onion, about 2 medium

3 tbsp. light mayonnaise

3 tbsp. grated Parmesan cheese

1 tsp. minced garlic

1. Put artichoke hearts, ricotta, sour cream, parsley, green onion, mayonnaise, Parmesan and garlic in a food processor; process until slightly chunky.

Cal 56 • Fat 3 g — Yield: 8 Servings

Tuna Cannellini Bean Spread

Combining tuna with cannellini beans is an Italian tradition. This spread is best served on grilled or toasted slices of crusty Italian or French bread. Add a little pizzazz by topping with finely diced tomatoes or chopped fresh basil leaves.

6½ oz. can solid white tuna packed in water, drained

1 cup canned cannellini beans, rinsed well and drained (great Northern OR navy beans can be substituted for cannellini)

1 garlic clove, minced

1 tsp. dried basil

¼ tsp. dried oregano

1 tsp. olive oil

1 tbsp. + 1 tsp. red wine vinegar

⅛ tsp. salt

6 kalamata olives, pitted and sliced

1. In a small bowl, break up tuna with a fork. Add beans and mash roughly. Stir in the remaining ingredients. Serve at room temperature.

Cal 59 • Fat 0 g

Yield: 12 Servings

No-Guilt Guacamole

When bigger is better. For half the fat and 35% fewer calories, try a Florida avocado. This larger, smooth-skinned variety has a silkier texture and flavor, and often costs less than the California variety. Look for the SlimCado label, available June through February. Peas sneak in to add texture and color while reducing fat and calories.

1 avocado

¼ cup frozen peas, thawed

1 tbsp. lime juice

1 medium tomato, quartered

¼ cup chopped onion

1 tsp. minced garlic

1-2 tbsp. fresh cilantro leaves

1 small jalapeño chile pepper, seeded

½ tsp. ground cumin

salt and pepper to taste

1. Cut avocado in half lengthwise around the seed. Scoop the flesh into a bowl.
2. Add peas, lime juice, tomato, onion, garlic, cilantro, chile pepper and cumin. Add salt and pepper to taste.
3. Place mixture in a food processor or blender and pulse to the desired consistency.

Cal 55 • Fat 3 g

Yield: 4 Servings

Avocado Tomato Salsa

Serve with crackers or pita crisps. For an authentic, intense flavor, use ½ tsp. finely diced chile pepper or more chile powder.

2 cups finely chopped plum tomatoes

½ cup finely chopped avocado, ripe yet firm

⅓ cup chopped fresh coriander

¼ cup chopped green onion

1 tbsp. olive oil

1 tbsp. lime OR lemon juice

1 tsp. minced garlic

⅛ tsp. chile powder

1. In a bowl, combine tomatoes, avocado, coriander, green onion, olive oil, lime juice, garlic and chile powder.
2. Allow salsa to marinate for 2 hours before serving.

Cal 53 • Fat 4 g Yield: 8 Servings

Corn & Tomato Salsa

Very simple but full of flavor – make at least 2 hours before using.

4 ears of corn, husks and silk removed

2 cups chopped tomatoes

½ cup apple cider vinegar

2 tbsp. sugar

salt and pepper to taste (optional)

⅓ cup chopped cilantro

1. Cook corn in boiling water 3 to 5 minutes, or until tender. Remove kernels from cobs with a sharp knife.

2 In a large saucepan, simmer corn kernels, tomatoes, cider vinegar, sugar, salt and pepper for 15 minutes. Stir in cilantro. Ladle salsa into jars. Cover and refrigerate for up to 2 months.

Cal 31 • Fat 0 g Yield: 16 Servings

Marinated Broccoli Appetizer

Grapefruit juice adds zesty tang.

1 cup broccoli florets, blanched
¼ cup grapefruit juice
1 tbsp. chopped scallion
2 tsp. vegetable oil
½ tsp. salt
dash EACH salt and pepper
2 large lettuce leaves, formed into cups

1. Combine all ingredients, except lettuce, in a small bowl; toss well. Cover and refrigerate at least 2 hours or overnight.
2. Serve in lettuce cups.

Cal 86 • Fat 5 g — Yield: 2 Servings

Rutabaga Appetizer

A cross between a cabbage and a turnip, rutabagas are often called Swedish turnips – they are pale yellow with a slightly sweet flavor.

¼ cup pared and grated rutabaga
1 tsp. vegetable oil
½ tsp. sugar
½ tsp. red wine vinegar
⅛ tsp. salt
dash white pepper
½ cup lettuce leaves
1 parsley sprig
1 cherry tomato, halved

1. In a bowl, combine all ingredients, except lettuce, parsley and tomato.
2. Line a salad plate with lettuce leaves; top with rutabaga mixture. Garnish with parsley and tomato halves.

Cal 74 • Fat 5 g — Yield: 1 Serving

Bacon-Stuffed Deviled Eggs

Packed with flavor from bacon, scallion and a touch of hot sauce, our version of this beloved summer dish is so simple yet it tastes amazing!

6 eggs

2 slices bacon

¼ cup light mayonnaise

¼ tsp. salt

⅛ tsp. pepper

⅛ tsp. hot sauce, such as Tabasco

1 scallion, finely chopped

1. In a large saucepan over high heat, combine eggs with enough cold water to cover by 1"; bring to a boil. Cover. Remove from heat; let stand 15 minutes. Drain. Cover eggs with cold water. When cool, peel; halve lengthwise.
2. Meanwhile, in a nonstick skillet over medium-high heat, cook bacon until crisp, 6-8 minutes; drain on paper towels. When bacon is cool, chop finely.
3. Place yolks in a bowl. Using a fork, stir in mayonnaise, salt, pepper and hot sauce until smooth. Stir in scallion and all but 1 tbsp. of bacon. If desired, transfer yolk mixture to a pastry bag fitted with a large star tip. Pipe or, using small spoon, mound yolk mixture into each egg white. Sprinkle with remaining bacon.

Cal 60 • Fat 5 g

Yield: 12 Servings

Roasted Red Pepper Pesto Toasts

Roasted red peppers have a luscious rich flavor. They are also high in vitamins C and A – by weight, red peppers have 3 times as much vitamin C as citrus fruit.

3 tbsp. bottled pesto

7 oz. bottle roasted red bell peppers, drained

¼ tsp. salt

¼ tsp. black pepper

16 (¼" thick) baguette slices

16 fresh flat-leaf parsley leaves

1. Preheat oven to 350°F.
2. Place pesto, peppers, salt and pepper in a food processor; process until smooth. Spread 2 tsp. of pesto mixture evenly over each bread slice.
3. Place bread slices on an ungreased baking sheet and bake for 10 minutes. Garnish each slice with 1 parsley leaf.

Pictured on page 67.

Cal 74 • Fat 2.3 g Yield: 16 Servings

Hot Mushroom Turnovers

A hot and savory taste sensation.

½ cup + 2 tbsp. enriched flour
¼ tsp. salt
2 tbsp. + 2 tsp. margarine
¼ cup plain unflavored yogurt

Mushroom Filling

1½ cups minced mushrooms
1 tbsp. dehydrated onion flakes
1 tbsp. chopped fresh parsley
¼ tsp. Worcestershire sauce
1 garlic clove, minced
dash EACH thyme leaves, salt and pepper

1. Combine flour and salt in mixing bowl. Cut in margarine until mixture resembles a coarse meal. Add yogurt and mix thoroughly. Form dough into a ball and chill about 1 hour.
2. **Filling**: Combine remaining ingredients in a nonstick skillet; cook until mushrooms are soft and all moisture has evaporated.
3. Preheat oven to 375°F.
4. Roll out dough to about ⅛" thickness. With a pastry wheel, cut lengthwise strips 2½" apart, then cut crosswise, making 2½" squares. Re-roll scraps of dough, cutting until all dough is used. Place an equal amount of mushroom mixture on each square, about 1 tsp. Fold in half to enclose filling and form a triangle; seal well, pressing edges together with fork tines.
5. Bake on an ungreased baking sheet 20 to 25 minutes, or until lightly browned.

Cal 77 • Fat 4 g   Yield: 8 Servings

Portobello Mushrooms with Thyme & Shallots

Portobellos are larger, more mature dark brown cremino mushrooms – related to white button mushrooms, their flavor is a bit richer and the texture is more firm.

4 large portobello mushrooms (about 1 lb.)
nonstick spray
1 tsp. olive oil
½ cup finely diced red bell pepper
¼ cup finely diced shallots
½ tsp. salt
¼ tsp. freshly ground black pepper
2 tsp. chopped fresh thyme or ½ tsp. dried
1 cup toasted bread crumbs
¼ cup shredded Asiago OR Romano cheese

1. Preheat oven to 375°F.
2. Clean mushrooms; remove stems. Finely chop stems. Using a paring knife, scrape out and discard gills from caps. Coat both sides of caps with nonstick spray. Arrange caps rounded side down on a jelly-roll pan or baking sheet.
3. Heat oil in a large nonstick skillet over medium heat. Add chopped mushroom stems, bell pepper, shallots, salt and pepper; cook 5 minutes, stirring occasionally. Stir in thyme; spoon mixture into mushroom caps. Combine bread crumbs and cheese; sprinkle evenly over mushrooms. Coat crumb mixture with nonstick spray. Bake 12 to 14 minutes, or until crumbs are golden brown and mushrooms are tender.

Cal 101 • Fat 4 g | Yield: 4 Servings

Crispy Oven-Fried Onion Rings

We all love onion rings – these are lower fat with great flavor.

1½ tsp. oil

1 medium onion

¼ cup fat-free egg substitute

¼ cup Italian-style seasoned bread crumbs

nonstick spray

1. Preheat oven to 350°F.
2. Spread 1½ tsp. oil over the bottom of a 9" pie plate. Slice onion and separate it into rings.
3. Put fat-free egg substitute in a shallow medium bowl and put bread crumbs in another shallow medium bowl. Dip onion rings in egg mixture; remove with a slotted spoon or your fingers and place in bread crumbs, turning to coat well.
4. Place onion rings in the prepared pan and coat tops generously with nonstick spray. Bake 15 minutes. Flip rings over and bake 10 minutes more, or until lightly browned and crisp.

Cal 102 • Fat 2 g

Yield: 4 Servings

Sauté of Summer Squash with Tomatoes & Garlic

Smaller, brightly colored summer squash are the best choices. They are high in vitamins A, C and niacin.

1 lb. assorted summer squash such as pattypan, sunburst, (yellow pattypan), globe (ronde de nice), zucchini (yellow and green) and cocozelle (Italian vegetable marrow)

1 tsp. olive oil

4 garlic cloves, thinly sliced

4 roma, plum or other small tomatoes, cut into ½" thick wedges

½ tsp. salt

¼ tsp. freshly ground black pepper

¼ cup grated Parmigiano-Reggiano OR Pecorino Romano cheese

1. Trim and cut squash crosswise into ½" thick slices.
2. Heat a large, deep nonstick skillet or sauté pan over medium heat. Add oil, then garlic; cook until edges of garlic just begin to turn golden, about 3 minutes, stirring frequently. Add squash; cook 5 minutes, or until squash is crisp-tender, stirring frequently. Add tomatoes, salt and pepper. Cook 2 minutes, or until squash is tender and tomatoes are hot, stirring occasionally.
3. Transfer to serving plates; top with cheese. Serve warm or at room temperature.

Cal 71 • Fat 3 g — Yield: 4 Servings

Green Bean & Red Cabbage Appetizer

The flavors of garlic and ginger make this colorful appetizer irresistible.

2 tsp. olive oil

½ cup diagonally sliced green beans, ½" pieces

½ garlic clove, chopped with ½ tsp. salt

½ tsp. minced fresh ginger

2 cups thinly sliced red cabbage

¼ tsp. salt

⅛ tsp. celery seeds

dash ground marjoram

½ tsp. lemon juice

1. Heat oil in a medium skillet. Add green beans, garlic and ginger. Sauté over medium heat until beans are just tender-crisp, about 2 to 3 minutes. **Do not overcook**. Remove beans from pan and keep warm.
2. Add cabbage, salt, celery seeds and marjoram to skillet. Cook, stirring occasionally, just until cabbage is tender. Stir in lemon juice. Return beans to skillet and stir to combine with cabbage.

Cal 81 • Fat 5 g

Yield: 2 Servings

Moroccan Lentil-Stuffed Peppers

Colorful, delicious and nutritious!

4 large bell peppers, preferably a mix of yellow, red, purple and orange

1 tbsp. olive oil

1 large leek, white and light green part thinly sliced

4 garlic cloves, minced

1 tsp. ground cumin

1 tsp. ground coriander

½ tsp. salt

¼ tsp. cinnamon

¼ tsp. cayenne pepper

1¾ cups fat-free low-sodium chicken broth

1 cup red lentils

15 oz. can chickpeas (garbanzo beans), drained

3 tbsp. chopped cilantro OR mint

1. Cut ½" off tops of bell peppers. Chop pepper tops, discarding stems; set aside. Remove seeds from peppers. Blanch peppers in boiling water or cook, covered, in microwave oven until tender (about 4 minutes in boiling water or at high power in microwave oven). Drain and set aside.

2. Heat a large saucepan over medium-high heat. Add oil, then chopped pepper tops, leek and garlic; sauté 4 minutes. Sprinkle cumin, coriander, salt, cinnamon and cayenne pepper over vegetables; mix well. Add broth and lentils; bring to a boil. Reduce heat; cover and simmer until lentils are tender and most of liquid is absorbed, about 16 minutes. Stir in chickpeas; heat through. Spoon filling into pepper bottoms. Serve immediately or reheat in 375°F oven or microwave oven.

   Garnish with cilantro or mint.

Cal 347 • Fat 6 g — Yield: 4 Servings

SALADS

Caesar Salad

This variation of Caesar salad is dramatically lower in fat and calories than the traditional recipe but with all of the flavor.

9 cups romaine lettuce torn into bite-sized pieces

½ cup nonfat yogurt

2 tsp. lemon juice

2 tsp. balsamic vinegar

1 tsp. Worcestershire sauce

1 small clove garlic, minced

½ tsp. anchovy paste

½ cup grated Parmesan cheese

1. Place lettuce in a large salad bowl.
2. In a blender or food processor, purée yogurt, lemon juice, vinegar, Worcestershire sauce, garlic, anchovy paste and ¼ cup of Parmesan until smooth.
3. Pour dressing over lettuce and toss well.
4. Sprinkle with remaining ¼ cup Parmesan and toss again. Serve on individual plates.

Cal 46 • Fat 1.4 g Yield: 6 Servings

Greek Feta Salad

Oregano is a classic Greek/Mediterranean culinary herb – the name means mountain joy. Oregano was used by ancient Greeks to treat many medical conditions, and current health studies show that fresh oregano has 40 times the antioxidant power of apples, 30 times that of potatoes and 12 times more than oranges or blueberries.

2 Little Gem lettuces

3 tomatoes, cut into wedges

1 green pepper, seeded and cut into thin slices

½ cucumber, quartered lengthwise and thickly sliced

7 oz. feta cheese

1 small red onion, finely sliced

12 black olives

Dressing

4 tbsp. extra-virgin olive oil

1 tbsp. lemon juice

1 tsp. chopped fresh oregano

lemon slices, to serve (optional)

1. Tear lettuce into bite-sized pieces and put in a large bowl or 4 individual bowls. Add tomato wedges, green pepper and cucumber.
2. Break feta cheese into small pieces and pile them in the middle. Top with onion and olives.
3. Whisk oil and lemon juice with oregano and spoon over salad before serving. Add lemon slices, if using.

Pictured on page 117.

Cal 290 • Fat 23 g — Yield: 4 Servings

Four-Tomato Salad

Any combination of tomatoes can be used if those specified here are not available. Yellow, larger tomatoes, if available, are great to add. Removing seeds from field tomatoes will eliminate excess liquid. Do not toss this salad until just ready to serve.

½ cup sun-dried tomatoes (NOT oil packed)

2 cups sliced field tomatoes

2 cups halved red OR yellow cherry tomatoes

2 cups quartered plum tomatoes

1 cup sliced red onion

⅓ cup chopped fresh basil or 2 tbsp. dried

Dressing

3 tbsp. olive oil

¼ cup balsamic vinegar

1½ tsp. minced garlic

⅛ tsp. ground black pepper

1. Pour boiling water over sundried tomatoes. Let rest for 15 minutes, until softened. Drain and chop.
2. Place sun-dried tomatoes, field tomatoes, cherry tomatoes, plum tomatoes, red onions and fresh basil in a serving bowl or on a platter.
3. Whisk together oil, vinegar, garlic and pepper; pour over tomatoes.

Pictured on page 169.

Cal 134 • Fat 8 g

Yield: 6 Servings

Cauliflower Salad

Cauliflower is related to broccoli and cabbage and tastes great in a marinated salad. It's also high in vitamin C.

2 cups cauliflower florets
2 cups boiling water
½ tsp. salt
1 tbsp. + 1½ tsp. white wine vinegar
4 black olives, pitted and diced
2 tbsp. diced pimiento strips
2 tsp. olive oil
dash each salt and pepper

1. Cook cauliflower in boiling salted water 6 minutes, or until tender-crisp; drain and transfer to a bowl.
2. Add vinegar and toss to coat; chill 30 minutes.
3. Add remaining ingredients and toss to combine.

Cal 87 • Fat 7 g Yield: 2 Servings

Coleslaw Vinaigrette

I can't say enough good things about cabbage. This is best made a few hours ahead as the flavor is enhanced as it marinates.

¼ cup cider vinegar
2 tbsp. + 2 tsp. vegetable oil
1 tsp. celery seed
¼ tsp. powdered mustard
dash garlic powder
2 cups shredded cabbage
¼ cup grated carrot
¼ cup diced green bell pepper

1. In a medium bowl, using a wire whisk, combine vinegar, oil, celery seed, mustard and garlic powder.
2. Add remaining ingredients; toss well.

Cal 112 • Fat 10 g Yield: 4 Servings

Fruit Slaw

4 cups shredded cabbage
1 small apple, cored and cut into small pieces
1 tbsp. raisins
1 tbsp. sesame seeds, toasted, divided
½ cup plain unflavored yogurt
¼ cup canned crushed pineapple, no sugar added
2 tbsp. reduced-calorie mayonnaise
1 tbsp. lemon juice

1. In a large bowl, combine cabbage, apple, raisins and 2 tsp. sesame seeds.
2. In a small bowl, combine remaining ingredients, except sesame seeds.
3. Add to cabbage mixture; toss to combine. Cover and chill overnight. Sprinkle with 1 tsp. sesame seeds just before serving.

Cal 106 • Fat 4 g Yield: 4 Servings

Coleslaw with Pineapple

Coleslaw with a tropical touch. Use water chestnuts if jicama is not available.

3 cups shredded cabbage
½ cup shredded carrots
1 cup jicama, peeled and cut into matchstick-sized pieces
1 green onion, chopped
12 oz. can crushed pineapple, drained (reserve ¼ cup juice)
¼ cup fat-free mayonnaise
¼ tsp. ground black pepper
¼ tsp. salt
2 tbsp. sunflower seeds

1. In a medium bowl, combine cabbage, carrots, jicama, green onion and drained pineapple. Set aside.
2. In small bowl, combine ¼ cup pineapple juice, mayonnaise, pepper and salt. Whisk until smooth and add to cabbage mixture. Add sunflower seeds and mix well. Let sit at least 1 hour before serving

Cal 40 • Fat 1 g Yield: 12 Servings

Extra-Creamy Coleslaw

This is my Fav-o-rite coleslaw. If you like KFC coleslaw, you'll love this!

⅓ cup sugar

½ tsp. salt

⅛ tsp. freshly ground pepper

¼ cup 1% milk

½ cup Hellmann's low-fat mayonnaise

¼ cup low-fat buttermilk

1½ tbsp. white vinegar

2½ tbsp. lemon juice

8 cups very finely chopped cabbage (about 1 medium head)

1 cup grated carrot

1. In a large bowl, combine sugar, salt, pepper, milk, mayonnaise, buttermilk, vinegar and lemon juice and beat with an electric mixer until smooth. (Or combine in a food processor and process until smooth, then transfer to a large bowl.)
2. Add cabbage and carrots and toss to blend with dressing. Cover and refrigerate for at least 3 hours before serving.

Cal 88 • Fat 1.4 g Yield: 8 Servings

Curried Coleslaw

Curry powder adds zest to this lively coleslaw – add it to taste.

2 cups shredded cabbage
1/4 cup chopped green bell pepper
1/4 cup chopped carrot
1/4 tsp. salt
1/8 tsp. celery seed
dash pepper
1/3 cup water
1/4 cup cider vinegar
2 tsp. dehydrated onion flakes
1 tsp. lemon juice
1/8 tsp. curry powder

1. Combine cabbage, green pepper, carrot, salt, celery seed and pepper in a medium bowl; set aside.
2. Combine remaining ingredients in a small bowl and let stand 5 minutes; add to cabbage mixture.
3. Toss and refrigerate at least 2 hours. Toss again just before serving.

Cal 44 • Fat 0.3 g   Yield: 2 Servings

Crunchy Cabbage Salad

This crunchy salad is from southern India. Enjoy it as a side dish or all by itself.

3 cups finely shredded green cabbage

1 tsp. olive oil

½ tsp. black OR yellow mustard seeds

½ tsp. turmeric

½ tsp. granulated white sugar

½ tsp. salt, or to taste

1 tbsp. coarsely ground unsalted peanuts (optional)

1 tbsp. lemon juice

1. Place cabbage in a medium-sized mixing bowl and set aside.
2. Place oil in a small skillet over medium-high heat. When oil is hot, add mustard seeds. Cover skillet with a splatter guard and allow seeds to pop. When seeds have finished popping (within 30 seconds), add turmeric and remove from the heat. Add this tempered oil to the shredded cabbage and stir well.
3. Add sugar, salt and peanuts, if using. Mix well.
4. Stir in lemon juice just before serving.

Cal 16 • Fat 0.8 g Yield: 6 Servings

Potato Salad

Fresh lemon and yogurt give this potato salad a refreshing, tart flavor.

1½ lbs. waxy, firm new potatoes, scrubbed

1 small lemon, zest and 2 tbsp. juice

Yogurt Dill Dressing

⅔ cup plain unflavored yogurt

2 tbsp. light mayonnaise

4 spring onions, trimmed and finely chopped

3 tbsp. chopped or torn fresh dillweed

salt and freshly ground black pepper

lemon wedges, to serve (optional)

1. Cook potatoes for 10 to 12 minutes in boiling salted water, until just tender. Drain well; cool under running water.
2. Place potatoes in a bowl and toss with lemon zest and juice. Leave to cool.
3. **Dressing**: Mix dressing ingredients together in a large bowl.
4. Halve, slice or dice potatoes and mix into dressing. Cover and chill before serving.
5. Serve with lemon wedges, if using.

Cal 117 • Fat 2 g

Yield: 6 Servings

Classic Creamy Potato Salad

This light version of the summertime classic is perfect for a picnic or a buffet table.

Creamy Dijon Dressing

½ cup Hellmann's light mayonnaise

¼ cup Hellmann's low-fat mayonnaise

¼ cup light sour cream

1 tbsp. vinegar, try tarragon, white OR cider

1½ tsp. Dijon mustard

½ tsp. dried parsley flakes

¼ tsp. dried thyme or 1 tsp. finely chopped fresh thyme

2 tsp. sugar

1 tsp. salt

¼ tsp. freshly ground pepper, or to taste

6 medium potatoes, peeled, cooked and cubed (about 5 cups)

1 cup sliced celery

½ cup chopped onion

2 hard-cooked egg whites, chopped

1. **Dressing**: In a large bowl, combine mayonnaises, sour cream, vinegar, mustard, parsley, thyme, sugar, salt and pepper.
2. Add potatoes, celery, onion and chopped egg whites. Toss to coat well.
3. Cover and chill in the refrigerator until ready to serve.

Cal 243 • Fat 5.5 g Yield: 8 Servings

Greek Barley Salad

A great variation on traditional Greek salad. Remove tomato seeds to eliminate excess liquid. Prepare early in the day and refrigerate until ready to use.

3 cups chicken stock OR water
¾ cup barley
1½ cups diced cucumber
1½ cups diced tomato
¾ cup chopped red onion
¾ cup chopped green pepper
⅓ cup sliced black olives
2 oz. feta cheese, crumbled

Citrus Vinaigrette

2 tbsp. olive oil
2 tbsp. lemon juice
1½ tsp. minced garlic
⅓ cup chopped fresh oregano

1. In medium saucepan, bring stock or water to boil; add barley. Cover, reduce heat and simmer for 40 to 45 minutes, or just until tender. Drain well and rinse with cold water.
2. Place barley in large serving bowl. Add cucumber, tomato, onion, green pepper, olives and feta cheese; toss well.
3. **Vinaigrette**: In small bowl, whisk together oil, lemon juice, garlic and oregano.
4. Pour dressing over salad and toss well. Refrigerate until chilled.

Cal 197 • Fat 8 g

Yield: 6 Servings

Chicken with Prawns, Mango and Orange Salad, page 38

Chickpea Salad

Make this salad a few hours ahead of time to let the vegetables marinate. Use parsley instead of cilantro if you prefer. Fresh herbs are a great way to flavor foods. Cilantro or Chinese parsley is fresh coriander and has a distinct aroma. Some people find cilantro has a strong taste, so you may want to use it in small amounts.

19 oz. can chickpeas, drained and rinsed
2 tomatoes, chopped
1 long English cucumber, diced
1 red bell pepper, chopped
½ purple onion, finely chopped
2 tbsp. chopped cilantro
1 tbsp. olive oil
3 tbsp. red wine vinegar
1 garlic clove, crushed
½ tsp. salt
¼ tsp. freshly ground black pepper

1. Combine chickpeas, tomatoes, cucumber, red pepper, onion and cilantro in a bowl. Set aside.
2. Combine oil, vinegar, garlic, salt and pepper in a jar. Shake well.
3. Pour dressing over vegetables and toss well. Chill before serving.

Cal 152 • Fat 4 g

Yield: 6 Servings

Tabbouleh with a Tang

Mint makes meals easy to digest. Menthol, the volatile oil found in mint, is a stomach-soothing compound that aids in digestion.

10 oz. pkg. couscous, like Near East

2 cups (16 oz.) yellow and /or red grape tomatoes, halved

1 cucumber, diced

1 cup chopped fresh mint

2 tbsp. prepared citrus vinaigrette, see page 32

salt, pepper, fresh lemon juice and hot pepper sauce (optional)

1. Prepare couscous according to package directions. Fluff with a fork.
2. In a large bowl, toss together couscous, tomatoes, cucumber, mint and citrus vinaigrette.
2. Season with salt, pepper, extra lemon juice and hot pepper sauce to taste, if desired. Chill.

Cal 176 • Fat 3 g

Yield: 4 Servings

Chicken Tabbouleh

Tabbouleh – the Middle Eastern salad of bulgur (steamed, dried, crushed wheat), tomatoes, fresh parsley and mint.

1 cup medium-coarse bulgur
2 cups boiling water
¾ cup diced dried apricots
½ cup pineapple juice
½ cup chicken broth, canned
½ lb. skinless, boneless chicken breast, cut into ¼" dice
2 cups shredded carrots
1½ cups chopped parsley, preferably flat-leaf
¼ cup finely sliced scallion
3 tbsp. fresh lemon juice
1 tbsp. + 1 tsp. extra-virgin olive oil
¾ tsp. freshly ground black pepper
½ tsp. salt
2 medium tomatoes, sliced

1. In a medium bowl, combine bulgur and water. Let stand for 30 minutes; drain, pressing out excess water.
2. In a small bowl, combine apricots and pineapple juice; let stand.
3. In a small saucepan over high heat, bring chicken broth to a boil. Add chicken; reduce heat to medium; simmer, stirring frequently until chicken is cooked, 3 to 5 minutes. Transfer chicken to a plate; cover loosely.
4. Over high heat, reduce broth until caramel-colored and syrupy, to about 1 tbsp., about 10 minutes. Set aside.
5. In a large bowl, combine bulgur, apricots and liquid, chicken, carrots, parsley and scallions. Toss well.
6. In a small bowl, whisk broth with lemon juice, oil, pepper and salt. Pour dressing over salad; toss well.
7. Mound salad on a platter; surround with tomatoes.

Cal 347 • Fat 6.5 g　　Yield: 4 Servings

Chicken with Prawns, Mango & Orange Salad

This is an easily prepared summer salad with the typical Thai sour and slightly sweet flavors, very refreshing with the fruit and not high in fat.

2 tbsp. vegetable oil

2 to 3 garlic cloves, peeled, cut into thin slivers

2 shallots OR 1 small onion, peeled and thinly sliced

2 chicken breasts (about 12 oz.), skinned and boned

8 to 12 raw prawns, peeled, tails on

1 tsp. EACH salt and sugar

3 to 4 tbsp. lime juice

1 medium orange

1 mango

2 to 3 hot green chiles cut into thin rounds (seeded, if preferred)

frisée lettuce leaves

a good handful of fresh coriander leaves

2 oz. roasted cashew nuts OR peanuts

Thai fish sauce, to serve with salad

1. Heat oil in a pan; fry garlic and shallots until golden. Drain in a sieve, then on paper towels.
2. Add chicken breasts to a pan of simmering salted water and cook for about 20 minutes, until tender, then add prawns and simmer for 2 minutes. Drain and cool. Tear chicken into shreds.
3. Mix salt with sugar and lime juice in a small bowl.
4. Segment orange, adding juice to lime juice. Peel and slice mango. Toss chicken strips and prawns in fruit juice in a large bowl, then add orange and mango. Add rounds of chile.
5. Arrange some frisée lettuce leaves on individual plates; spoon the salad on top. Sprinkle with fried garlic and shallots, coriander leaves and roasted cashews. Serve with a dish of Thai fish sauce and any leftover garlic and shallots.

Pictured on page 33.

Cal 300 • Fat 16 g | Yield: 4 Servings

Caribe Turkey Salad

Fresh fruit and turkey make a satisfying and thoroughly beautiful salad.

16 large Romaine lettuce leaves

1 papaya, peeled, seeded and cut into thin slices

3 cups quartered strawberries

2 kiwi fruit, peeled and cut into thin slices

1 lb. roast turkey breast, cut into ½" cubes

¼ cup dry-roasted cashews OR peanuts, diced

Caribe Dressing

⅓ cup frozen tropical fruit-juice-blend concentrate, thawed

¼ cup rice wine vinegar

1 tbsp. olive oil

1. Arrange lettuce on 4 individual serving plates. Top with papaya, strawberries and kiwi fruit. Mound the turkey in the center. Sprinkle with nuts.
2. **Dressing**: In a small bowl or screw-top jar, combine fruit juice concentrate, vinegar and oil. Whisk or shake to blend.
3. Pour dressing over salads and serve.

Cal 375 • Fat 9 g

Yield: 4 Servings

Basic Vinaigrette

1 tbsp. + 1 tsp. olive OR vegetable oil

1 tbsp. white wine vinegar

⅛ tsp. EACH salt and prepared mustard

Combine all ingredients in a small bowl; mix well.

VARIATIONS:

Chile Vinaigrette

Add 2 tsp. chile sauce to Basic Vinaigrette.

Cal 45 • Fat 5 g

Cider Vinaigrette

Substitute cider vinegar for wine vinegar in Basic Vinaigrette.

Cal 42 • Fat 5 g

Garlic Vinaigrette

Prepare Basic vinaigrette; **omit salt**. With flat side of knife **mash ¼ small garlic clove with ⅛ tsp. salt** to form a paste. Add paste to dressing.

Cal 43 • Fat 5 g

Gingered Vinaigrette

Add ¼ tsp. minced fresh ginger to Basic Vinaigrette.

Cal 42 • Fat 5 g

Oregano Vinaigrette

Substitute oregano vinegar for wine vinegar in Basic Vinaigrette.

Cal 42 • Fat 5 g

Cal 42 • Fat 5 g Servings 4

SOUPS

Cold Blueberry Soup

Blueberries are so great for you, full of antioxidants and flavor, mmmm.

1 cup blueberries

1 cup water, divided

⅔ cup grape juice, no sugar added

1 tbsp. honey

2 tsp. cornstarch

1. Combine blueberries, ¾ cup water, grape juice and honey in a medium saucepan; cover and simmer over low heat until berries are soft, about 5 minutes. Do not overcook.
2. Dissolve cornstarch in remaining ¼ cup water; stir dissolved cornstarch into soup and cook, stirring occasionally, until mixture thickens enough to coat back of spoon.
3. Remove soup from heat; cool and refrigerate, covered, until well chilled.

Cal 55 • Fat 0.2 g

Yield: 4 Servings

Cold Curried Mango Soup

A ripe mango should give slightly to the touch and have a splendid, full aroma. In general, mangoes are most affordable, available and at their peak of flavor during the late summer months, the very best time of all to make this exotic, cooling combination.

1 tsp. olive oil
1 small onion, diced
2 tsp. curry powder
½ cup chicken broth diluted with ½ cup water
3 large mangoes, peeled
1 tbsp. light brown sugar
½ tsp. ground ginger
¼ tsp. allspice
¼ tsp. salt
1¼ cups plain nonfat yogurt
½ cup water
2 tbsp. fresh lime juice
2 tbsp. minced fresh basil

1. In a small nonstick skillet, warm oil over medium heat until hot but not smoking. Add onion and curry powder; cook for 1 minute. Add ¼ cup of chicken broth and simmer gently until onion has softened, about 4 minutes.
2. Remove flesh from 2 mangoes and transfer to a food processor or blender along with onion mixture, brown sugar, ginger, allspice and salt. Process to a smooth purée. Add 1 cup of yogurt; remaining ¾ cup broth, the water and lime juice, and process to combine. Chill until ready to serve.
3. Before serving, cut remaining mango into ½" cubes. Spoon soup into 4 soup bowls; dollop with remaining ¼ cup yogurt, spoon diced mango on top and sprinkle basil over soup.

Cal 211 • Fat 2.2 g Yield: 4 Servings

Danish Apple Soup

Apples and cinnamon make a delicious soup – This is refreshing cold and comforting hot.

4 small apples

3 cups water, divided

1 tbsp. grated lemon zest

¾ tsp. ground cinnamon

1 tsp. sugar

½ tsp. salt

1 tbsp. cornstarch, dissolved in 1 tbsp. water

1 tbsp. + 1 tsp. Burgundy or other dry red wine

1. Pare and core 3 apples and cut each into eighths.
2. In a saucepan combine apples, water, lemon zest and cinnamon. Bring to a boil; reduce heat and simmer for 15 minutes. Add sugar and salt.
3. Transfer soup to a blender container; process until puréed.
4. Return soup to saucepan. Add remaining water; bring to a boil. Stirring constantly, gradually add dissolved cornstarch. Stir and cook until slightly thickened; stir in Burgundy.
5. Core remaining apple; cut into small dice and stir into soup. Serve chilled or hot .

Cal 83 • Fat 1 g   Yield: 4 Servings

Chilled Cucumber Soup

The longer this soup chills, the stronger the curry flavor will become – very cooling in hot weather.

1 medium cucumber, pared, seeded and sliced

¾ cup buttermilk

½ cup peeled and chopped tomato

1 tsp. chopped red onion

1 small garlic clove

¼ tsp. curry powder

¼ tsp. salt

dash pepper

1½ tsp. chopped fresh parsley

1. In a blender container, combine cucumber, buttermilk, tomato, onion and garlic. Process until mixture is smooth. Add curry powder, salt and pepper; process until combined.
2. Pour soup into a bowl; cover and chill about 1 hour. Sprinkle with chopped parsley before serving.

Cal 135 • Fat 2 g

Yield: 2 servings

Tomato Soup

This version of western India's classic spicy tomato soup is refreshing, flavorful and fat-free.

16 oz. can whole peeled tomatoes (no salt added)

1 tbsp. cornstarch

1 cup water

½ tsp. grated ginger

1 garlic clove, crushed

½ tsp. ground cumin

salt and pepper to taste

1 tbsp. brown sugar

dash of Tabasco sauce

1 tbsp. finely chopped fresh cilantro

1. Place all ingredients, except cilantro, in a blender container and process until well-blended.
2. Transfer mixture to a medium-sized pot. Bring to a boil, then reduce heat to low and simmer about 10 minutes, stirring occasionally.
3. Ladle into soup bowls; garnish with cilantro and serve.

Cal 39 • Fat 0 g

Yield: 4 Servings

Fresh Start Onion Soup

Caramelized onions give this soup its rich flavor. Fructose, also called fruit sugar, is sweeter than sucrose but contains half the calories. It can be used by diabetics and comes in both syrup and granulated forms.

4 to 6 garlic cloves, minced

5 to 6 cups onions, sliced into separate rings

¼ cup evaporated skim milk

5 cups water

½ cup Burgundy

3 tbsp. low-sodium soy sauce

1 tbsp. whole-wheat flour

1 tsp. granulated fructose

2 whole-wheat onion bagels, sliced lengthwise

4 tbsp. grated Parmesan cheese

1. Spray a large nonstick frying pan with nonstick spray. Sauté garlic and onion until onion is translucent and lightly browned. Add evaporated skim milk. Cook 5 more minutes.
2. Combine water, Burgundy, soy sauce, flour and fructose in a 4-quart saucepan. Bring to a boil, stirring to dissolve the fructose and flour. Add onion and garlic. Simmer 20 to 25 minutes.
3. Preheat oven to 425°F.
4. Lightly toast bagel. Ladle soup into 4 ovenproof bowls. Place 1 slice of bagel in each bowl. Sprinkle 1 tbsp. of Parmesan cheese in each bowl on top of the bagel.
5. Place bowls on a flat pan. Bake for 10 minutes, or until cheese is golden.

Pictured on page 67.

Cal 217 • Fat 1.5 g

Yield: 4 Servings

Broccoli & Cheese Soup

Hard to believe that a broccoli and cheese soup so creamy and delicious isn't loaded with fat. Sure to please!

1 cup chopped onion

1 garlic clove, minced

½ cup chopped celery

2½ cups low-sodium, reduced-fat chicken broth

3 cups broccoli florets

1 cup peeled, cubed potatoes

½ cup low-fat sour cream

¾ cup shredded reduced-fat sharp cheddar cheese (3 oz.)

½ tsp. EACH ground thyme, black pepper and "lite" Worcestershire sauce

¼ tsp. salt

4 to 5 dashes hot pepper sauce

1. Spray a large saucepan with nonstick spray. Add onion, garlic and celery. Cook and stir over medium heat until celery begins to soften, about 5 minutes. Add broth, 2 cups broccoli and all potatoes. Bring to a boil. Reduce heat to medium-low. Cover and simmer for 10 to 12 minutes, until broccoli and potatoes are tender.
2. While soup is simmering, steam reserved 1 cup broccoli until tender, about 5 minutes. Set aside.
3. Transfer soup to a blender or food processor, working in batches if necessary. Pulse on and off until soup is coarsely puréed (still kind of chunky). Return puréed soup to pot over low heat. Add steamed broccoli, sour cream, cheese, thyme, pepper, Worcestershire sauce, salt and hot pepper sauce. Stir until smooth. Serve immediately.

Cal 109 • Fat 3.4 g

Yield: 5 Servings

Cauliflower & Zucchini Soup

A mellow creamy soup without the cream – puréed vegetables combine well with the crunch of tender-crisp cauliflower florets and zucchini.

1 medium head cauliflower, about 1½ lbs.

5 cups water

1 cup sliced carrots

1 cup sliced celery

1 green pepper

½ bay leaf

1 medium zucchini, about 5 oz., halved and cut into 1" chunks

2 tsp. lemon juice

¾ tsp. salt

¼ tsp. dried thyme leaves

dash EACH ground allspice and nutmeg

1. Chop ⅔ of cauliflower; break remainder into florets and reserve.
2. In a medium saucepan, combine chopped cauliflower, water, carrots, celery, green pepper and bay leaf. Cover and bring to a boil. Reduce heat and simmer 30 minutes. Remove from heat and remove bay leaf.
3. Transfer mixture to a blender container and process until smooth; return to saucepan.
4. Add reserved florets and remaining ingredients; simmer, uncovered, stirring occasionally, 20 to 25 minutes, or until florets and zucchini are tender-crisp.

Cal 79 • Fat 0.5 g Yield: 4 Servings

Creamy Zucchini Soup

This soup is a delicious way to use up all of your fresh zucchini. Make several batches and freeze them for later use.

1½ cups beef broth

2 cups water

3 cups zucchini, peeled and sliced

½ cup chopped onion

⅛ tsp. garlic powder

salt to taste

3 cups skim milk

chives OR parsley, chopped, for garnish

1. Combine all ingredients, except milk and garnish, in a large saucepan. Cook until zucchini is tender.
2. Strain soup, reserving the liquid.
3. Purée zucchini mixture in a blender or put it through a food mill. Return to reserved liquid in saucepan.
4. Add milk and stir until smooth. Heat but do NOT boil.
5. Garnish with chives or parsley before serving.

Cal 71 • Fat Trace

Yield: 6 Servings

Potato Soup

Creamy and satisfying – a classic.

2 cups water

1 vegetable bouillon cube

4 medium potatoes, peeled and diced

1 medium onion, chopped

1 cup diced celery

1½ cups evaporated skim milk

⅛ tsp. pepper

⅛ tsp. nutmeg

1 tsp. soy sauce

2 tsp. dried dillweed

1. In a large saucepan, combine water, bouillon cube, potatoes, onion and celery.
2. Cover and cook over medium heat for 20 minutes, or until potatoes are soft.
3. Place vegetables in a blender or food processor. Purée.
4. Return purée to saucepan. Add remaining ingredients.
5. Heat soup through but do NOT boil.

Cal 116 • Fat 0 g

Yield: 6 Servings

Mushroom-Barley Soup

Dried mushrooms are the secret ingredient here. They add a rich, meaty flavor without an ounce of fat! Hearty barley complements their satisfying texture and flavor. This soup freezes well, so make a big batch and save some for later. Morgan's Favorite!

1 oz. dried mushrooms

3 cups water

1 large onion, chopped

2 carrots, chopped

1 celery stalk, chopped

12 oz. cremini OR button mushrooms, stems removed, sliced

1½ tsp. dried oregano

2, 14½ oz. cans fat-free, reduced-sodium chicken broth

½ cup barley

¼ tsp. salt

1. In a small saucepan, bring dried mushrooms and water to a boil. Remove and let stand for 15 minutes.
2. Meanwhile, coat a Dutch oven with nonstick spray. Add onion, carrots and celery. Cook over medium heat, stirring occasionally, for 3 minutes. Add cremini mushrooms and oregano. Cook, stirring occasionally, for 6 to 8 minutes, or until all vegetables are soft. Add broth, barley and salt. Cook for 10 minutes.
3. Line a fine mesh sieve with a coffee filter or paper towel. Strain dried mushroom water into the soup. Remove and discard filter. Rinse dried mushrooms under running water to remove any grit. Chop dried mushrooms and add to soup. Cook for 10 to 15 minutes, or until barley is tender.

Cal 148 • Fat 0 g — Yield: 6 Servings

Vegetable Soup

To vary the flavor, you can change the vegetables each time you make this chunky, light soup. Substitute 2 sliced leeks for the onion, watercress for the parsley, 1 1/2 cups diced rutabaga for the carrots, and peas and celery for the cabbage.

4 cups chicken stock

1 medium onion, quartered

1/4 cup chopped fresh parsley

1/4 cup chopped fresh dill

2 cups chopped celery

2 carrots, sliced

1 large sweet potato, cubed

1 large potato, cubed

1 large zucchini

1 bay leaf

4 cups torn fresh spinach, packed

2 cups shredded cabbage

salt and freshly ground pepper

1. In a large saucepan, bring chicken stock to a boil; add onion, parsley, dill, celery, carrots, potatoes, zucchini and bay leaf. Simmer, covered, until potatoes are tender, about 15 minutes. Remove bay leaf.
2. Add spinach and cabbage; cook, covered, for 5 to 7 minutes, or until cabbage is softened. Season with salt and pepper to taste.

Cal 99 • Fat 1.2 g

Yield: 6 Servings

24-Karat Gold Carrot Soup

What's up doc? This creamy decadent carrot soup is what's up. It's a #1 hitter – you'll love it! Healthy and delicious, what a combo.

6 cups low-sodium chicken broth

1½ cups coarsely chopped onion

3 garlic cloves, minced

3 tsp. grated ginger

4 cups coarsely chopped carrots

1½ tsp. ground thyme

½ cup pineapple juice

¾ cup buttermilk

5 drops hot pepper sauce

¼ tsp. cayenne (optional)

1 tbsp. chopped fresh parsley

1. Pour 1 cup chicken broth into a large saucepan. Add onion, garlic and ginger. Cook over medium-high heat for 3 minutes.
2. Stir in remaining broth, carrots, thyme and pineapple juice. Bring to a boil. Reduce heat to medium-low. Cover and boil gently for 20 minutes, or until carrots are tender.
3. Working in batches, transfer soup to a blender container and process until smooth. Return soup to saucepan. Reduce heat to low. Stir in buttermilk, hot pepper sauce and cayenne. Do not let soup boil. Stir until heated through, about 2 minutes.
4. Ladle into serving bowls and sprinkle with chopped fresh parsley.

Cal 99 • Fat 2 g

Yield: 6 Servings

Creamy Carrot Soup

Looking for a great meal opener? Here it is. The sweetness of carrot and orange is balanced by the tang of yogurt in this low-calorie soup. Yogurt will normally curdle if you add it to a soup or sauce, but blending with cornstarch solves the problem.

1 tbsp. vegetable oil

1 medium onion, chopped

1 large garlic clove, finely chopped

2 tsp. curry powder

4 cups sliced carrots

4 cups chicken stock

1 cup orange juice

1 cup plain low-fat yogurt

1 tbsp. cornstarch

salt and pepper

2 tbsp. chopped parsley OR chives

grated orange zest

1. In a large saucepan, heat oil over medium heat. Add onion, garlic and curry powder; cook, stirring, for 2 minutes, or until softened. Add carrots, chicken stock and orange juice. Bring to a boil; simmer, covered for 45 minutes, or until carrots are very tender. Let cool 10 minutes.
2. In a blender or food processor, purée soup in batches; return to saucepan.
3. In a bowl, blend yogurt and cornstarch; stir into soup. Cook over medium heat, stirring, for 5 minutes, or until heated through. Season to taste with salt and pepper.
4. Ladle into bowls; sprinkle with parsley and orange zest.

Cal 153 • Fat 4 g

Yield: 6 Servings

Borscht

This hearty beet soup is sure to put a smile on your face. Have it warm or cool, either way you'll enjoy it!

6 cups low-sodium beef broth

2½ cups coarsely grated beets

2½ cups shredded cabbage

2½ cups peeled, cubed potatoes

1 cup coarsely chopped red onion

2 tbsp. red wine vinegar

2 tbsp. chile sauce

1 tbsp. Worcestershire sauce

1 bay leaf

1 clove garlic, minced

½ tsp. dried dillweed

½ tsp. pepper

½ cup low-fat sour cream

¼ cup chopped fresh parsley

1. Combine all ingredients, except sour cream and parsley, in a large saucepan. Bring to a boil. Reduce heat to medium, cover and boil gently for 20 minutes, or until potatoes are tender. Stir occasionally. Remove from heat.
2. Measure sour cream into a 2-cup measuring cup. Add 1 cup of soup to the same cup. Blend until smooth. Add sour cream mixture to soup pot and stir well. Add parsley and stir again. Serve immediately or refrigerate and serve as a chilled summer soup.

Cal 115 • Fat 0.5 g

Yield: 6 Servings

Sweet Potato Soup

Sweet potatoes are classed as one of the worlds healthiest foods. The darker the variety, the higher the vitamin A concentration and lycopene. Sweet potatoes are also a very good source of vitamins C and B6, plus a good source of manganese, vitamin B2 and dietary fiber. They are also classed as "antidiabetic" – helping to stabilize blood sugar levels. Don't store sweet potatoes in the refrigerator – keep them in a cool, dark place.

2 large or 3 medium sweet potatoes, cooked, peeled

2¾ cups water

⅓ cup plain low-fat yogurt

½ cup dry cooking sherry

2 vegetable bouillon cubes

5 tbsp. grated Parmesan cheese

⅛ tsp. white pepper

1 tbsp. low-sodium soy sauce

1 tsp. dried dillweed

1. Scoop out pulp from cooked potatoes. Place pulp in a food processor with 1¾ cups water and yogurt. Purée.
2. Place purée in a saucepan with remaining water, sherry, and vegetable bouillon cube; heat over medium heat. Slowly add cheese, pepper, soy sauce and dillweed.
3. Bring to a boil, stirring constantly. Reduce heat to medium, stirring until soup thickens slightly, 10 to 15 minutes.

SOUPS

Cal 142 • Fat 1.7 g

Yield: 6 Servings

Butternut Squash Soup

The swirl of yogurt mellows out the powerful flavor of the spices. Macintosh apples are best in this soup, but any apples will work. Butternut squash is rich in vitamin C and beta-carotene. In fact, most squashes, including pumpkin, are high in these antioxidant vitamins.

2 tsp. oil

1 large onion, chopped

2 garlic cloves, minced

3 apples, peeled, cored and chopped

1 tbsp. minced fresh ginger

1 tbsp. curry powder

½ tsp. ground cumin

6 cups peeled, seeded and cubed butternut squash (2 lbs.)

4 cups chicken broth

1 cup apple juice

salt and ground black pepper to taste

½ cup nonfat plain yogurt (optional)

1. Heat oil in a large soup pot over medium heat. Add onion and sauté until softened. Add garlic and apples and sauté until apples are soft. Add ginger, curry powder and cumin; cook for 2 minutes. Add squash, chicken broth and apple juice. Bring to a boil. Reduce heat and simmer for 30 to 40 minutes, or until squash is tender.
2. Strain soup mixture and reserve liquid. Purée solids in a food processor or with a hand blender until smooth. Return liquid and puréed mixture to soup pot. Heat through. Season with salt and pepper and adjust spices. Add a dollop of yogurt to each bowl before serving, if desired.

Cal 141 • Fat 2 g

Yield: 8 Servings

Butternut-Bean Soup

Squash and white beans are flavored with curry and fresh ginger. This soup is very tasty and excellent for the metabolism.

¼ cup low-sodium nonfat chicken broth
1 medium onion, diced
1 cup diced celery
2 garlic cloves, crushed
1 jalapeño pepper, seeded and minced
1 tbsp. fresh grated ginger
4 cups peeled, chopped butternut squash
¼ cup minced fresh parsley
1 tsp. dried thyme
1 tbsp. curry powder
1 tsp. ground cumin
6 cups water
1 cup chopped spinach
1½ cups low-sodium canned Great Northern beans, drained and rinsed

1. Heat broth in a large saucepan. Add onion, celery, garlic, jalapeño pepper and ginger. Sauté over medium heat for 6 minutes.
2. Add squash and sauté for an additional 3 minutes. Stir in parsley, thyme, curry powder and cumin; sauté for 1 minute more.
3. Add water. Bring to a boil; reduce heat and simmer, stirring occasionally, for 20 minutes.
4. Stir in spinach and beans, and simmer for 10 more minutes. Transfer to individual bowls and serve.

SOUPS

Cal 78 • Fat 0 g

Yield: 10 Servings

Sunshine Soup

The rich golden color of this squash soup warms up any autumn meal.

2 cups squash, cooked, mashed
3 onions, chopped
1 cup chopped celery
1 garlic clove, minced
½ tsp. rosemary
4 cups chicken stock
¼ tsp. black pepper
2 cups skim milk
nutmeg for garnish

1. Combine all ingredients, except milk and nutmeg, in a large saucepan. Cook until onions and celery are tender.
2. Remove from heat; add milk and sprinkle with nutmeg. Serve immediately.

Cal 66 • Fat Trace

Yield: 6 Servings

Bean & Squash Soup

This soup freezes well.

2 tbsp. margarine
½ cup minced onion
1 small garlic clove, minced
1 quart water
24 oz. cooked great northern beans
1½ cups pared, cubed butternut squash
2 packets instant chicken broth and seasoning mix
2 tsp. minced fresh ginger
dash pepper

1. Melt margarine in a saucepan; add onion and garlic and sauté until softened. Add water, beans, squash, broth mix and ginger. Cook for 30 minutes, or until beans and squash are very soft.
2. Put soup through a food mill or purée in a food processor.

3 Reheat soup; add pepper. Stir in a little more water if soup is too thick.

Cal 291 • Fat 7 g

Yield: 4 Servings

Vegetable Minestrone

Every fall, when vegetables are at their prime, I make a double batch of this soup. Packed into containers and stored in the freezer, it's an instant warming meal for chilly days. Any combination of vegetables can be used in this hearty soup – use up the odds and ends in your fridge.

1 tbsp. olive oil
2 large onions, chopped
3 garlic cloves, finely chopped
2 carrots, peeled and chopped
2 celery stalks, chopped
10 cups vegetable OR chicken stock (approximately)
2 cups shredded cabbage
2 cups small cauliflower florets
⅓ cup short fine noodles or other small pasta shapes
1 cup frozen peas
19 oz. can Romano OR navy beans, rinsed and drained
¼ cup chopped parsley
grated Parmesan cheese (optional)

1. In a large stockpot or Dutch oven, heat oil over medium heat. Add onions, garlic, carrots and celery. Cook, stirring occasionally, for 10 minutes, or until softened.
2. Add stock and cabbage; bring to a boil over high heat. Reduce heat; simmer, covered, for 20 minutes, or until vegetables are tender. Add cauliflower and pasta. Simmer, covered, for 8 minutes, or until pasta is tender. Add peas and beans; cook for 2 minutes.
3. Ladle soup into bowls; garnish with chopped parsley. If desired, sprinkle with Parmesan cheese. Soup will thicken as it cools; add more stock if necessary.

Cal 233 • Fat 4 g

Yield: 8 Servings

Easy Kidney Bean Soup

Fast, simple and tasty.

1 lb. cooked kidney beans (canned or dried)
2 cups tomato sauce
3 medium onions, coarsely chopped
3 celery stalks, chopped
2 garlic cloves, minced
1 tsp. EACH thyme and oregano
1 tbsp. low-sodium soy sauce
½ tsp. pepper
1 tsp. dried dillweed
7 cups water

1. Combine all ingredients in a large soup pot
2. Simmer for 1 hour.

Cal 80 • Fat 0.3 g Yield: 6 to 8 Servings

Hearty Lentil Soup

Vegetarians and folks watching their fat intake will love this high-fiber soup.

2 medium onions, chopped
2 celery stalks, chopped
4 carrots, chopped
2 parsnips, peeled and chopped
2 cloves garlic, minced
1½ cups brown lentils, rinsed, drained and cleaned
1 tsp. dried thyme
8 cups vegetable broth plus additional, if desired
salt and pepper (optional)

1. Combine all ingredients, except salt and pepper, in the container of a slow cooker. Cover and cook on high until the lentils are soft and the vegetables are tender, about 5 hours.
2. Add salt and pepper to taste, if desired. Add additional heated vegetable broth if the soup is too thick.

Cal 140 • Fat 0 g Yield: 8 Servings

Lentil Tomato Soup

So thick it could be called a stew. Use any vegetables you have on hand, such as zucchini, broccoli and green beans. Lentils are one of those power-packed foods that give us so much nutrition in just one portion. Not only are they a great source of protein and fiber, they are one of the best food sources of folic acid. Just 1 cup of cooked lentils contains 15 grams of fiber, 18 grams of protein and 350 micrograms of folic acid.

2,10 oz. cans chicken broth
2½ cups water
2 cups dried green lentils
1 medium onion
2 medium carrots, peeled
2 celery stalks
1 green bell pepper, seeded
1 red bell pepper, seeded
2 potatoes, peeled and diced
28 oz. can diced tomatoes
14 oz. can stewed tomatoes
1 tsp. curry powder

1. Place chicken broth and water in a large soup pot. Rinse lentils in cold water, drain and add to pot.
2. Finely chop onion, carrots, celery and peppers. Add to pot and cover. Bring to a boil; lower heat and simmer, covered, for 45 minutes, until lentils are tender.
3. Add potatoes, diced and stewed tomatoes and curry powder. Return to a boil and simmer for 30 minutes longer.

Pictured on page 67.

Cal 179 • Fat 1 g

Yield: 12 Servings

Hearty Split Pea Soup

This stouthearted soup is wholesome and nourishing enough to be the main course. Round out your meal with a big salad and a slice of whole-grain bread or high-fiber crackers.

2 cups dried split peas
2 oz. lean ham, diced
6 cups water
1 cup chopped carrots
½ cup chopped onion
½ cup chopped celery
¼ cup chopped celery leaves
1 tbsp. parsley flakes
1 tsp. basil
¼ tsp. allspice
¼ tsp. thyme
1 bay leaf

1. Place split peas and ham in a large soup pot. Add water.
2. Sauté carrots, onion and celery until tender. Add to split peas.
3. Stir in remaining ingredients. Bring to a boil; cover and simmer 30 minutes. Remove bay leaf. Serve soup.
4. Purée soup in a blender if a smoother consistency is desired.

Cal 90 • Fat 2 g Yield: 8 Servings

Mixed Legume Soup

This hearty soup, which calls for carrots, potato and spinach, makes an exotic and colorful dish. A real comfort soup.

¼ cup EACH dry yellow split peas, pigeon peas and split mung beans

2 medium carrots, cut into ½" circles

1 medium potato, peeled and cut into ½" cubes

1 cup thoroughly washed, chopped fresh spinach leaves, packed

½ tsp. grated ginger

¼ tsp. turmeric

1 tsp. ground cumin

½ tsp. ground coriander

¼ tsp. cayenne pepper

½ tsp. salt, or to taste

1. Pick through dried peas and beans for any grit or debris. Place them in a strainer and rinse thoroughly. Transfer to a medium-sized soup pot along with 2 cups of water. Soak for 2 hours. Drain.
2. Add 3 cups water to peas and beans and bring to a boil over high heat. Reduce heat to medium-low and continue cooking, partially covered, for 35 minutes, stirring occasionally. Add more water if necessary.
3. Add remaining ingredients and 1 cup water to the pot. Cook another 15 minutes. Remove pot from heat and allow soup to cool slightly.
4. Transfer soup to a blender and purée in batches. Return soup to pot and bring to a gentle boil over medium-high heat.
5. Ladle hot soup into individual bowls and serve.

Cal 152 • Fat 1.8 g — Yield: 5 Servings

Black-Eyed Pea Soup

Creamy white, with a black "eye", these soft-textured peas, also called cowpeas, are an excellent source of fiber and folate and a good source of iron. They are traditionally used in an African American dish called Hoppin John and in Southern recipes with rice and greens or tossed with chopped tomatoes in a vinaigrette.

12 oz. dried black-eyed peas

7 cups water

2 medium potatoes, peeled and diced

3 celery stalks, sliced

2 carrots, sliced

3 tbsp. low-sodium soy sauce

1 medium onion, chopped

2 garlic cloves, diced

¼ tsp. pepper

1 tsp. dried basil

1 tsp. dried dillweed

1. Rinse black-eyed peas well. Place in a large soup pot and cover with water by 1" (in addition to water listed in ingredients). Soak overnight. Drain off water.
2. Add 7 cups of water and remaining ingredients. Bring to a boil. Boil 2 minutes.
3. Reduce heat to medium-low. Simmer 1 to 2 hours, or until peas are tender. Stir occasionally, mashing peas and potatoes against sides of the pot to thicken soup.

Cal 134 • Fat 0.5 g   Yield: 8 to 10 Servings

Fresh Start Onion Soup, page 47
Lentil Tomato Soup, page 63
Roasted Red Pepper Toasts, page 14

Manhattan Clam Chowder

The key to making any successful clam chowder that calls for fresh clams is not to overcook them. Add the littlenecks to the soup base and cook them as directed, then serve immediately in wide shallow bowls, preferably with a crusty loaf of bread for soaking up the delicious broth.

1 cup canned chicken broth diluted with 1 cup water, OR 2 cups homemade chicken broth

2½ cups diced carrots

½ lb. peeled all-purpose potatoes, cut into ½" cubes

1 medium onion, diced

1 medium celery stalk with leaves, diced

2 garlic cloves, crushed

2 bay leaves

¾ tsp. thyme

½ tsp. freshly ground black pepper

⅛ tsp. celery seed

2,14½ oz. cans stewed tomatoes

2 dozen littleneck clams, well scrubbed

2 tbsp. chopped parsley, preferably flat-leaf

1. In a Dutch oven or flameproof casserole, combine broth, carrots, potatoes, onion, celery, garlic, bay leaves, thyme, pepper and celery seed. Cover and bring to a boil over high heat. Reduce heat to medium and simmer until vegetables are tender, about 8 minutes.
2. Add tomatoes and bring to a boil over high heat. Reduce heat to medium and simmer, uncovered, for 5 minutes to blend flavors.
3. Add clams, cover and cook over medium-low heat, stirring occasionally, until clams open, 6 to 8 minutes. Discard any clams that do not open. Stir in parsley and serve.

Cal 225 • Fat 1.8 g

Yield: 4 Servings

Mulligatawny Soup

This fiery hot soup from southern India literally means "spice water." Its heat comes from fresh green chile peppers, as well as ground black pepper. Covered tightly and stored in the refrigerator, this soup will keep up to 5 days.

2 tbsp. dry split pigeon peas (found in the specialty aisle of your grocery store), remove any grit; place in a strainer; rinse thoroughly

2 cups water

1 fresh red or green chile pepper, halved lengthwise

⅛ tsp. turmeric

1 large tomato, coarsely chopped

1. In a medium-sized saucepan, cover peas with water; soak for 2 hours.
2. Place saucepan with peas and soaking water over high heat. Add fresh chile and turmeric; bring to a boil. Reduce heat to medium-low; simmer, partially covered, for 30 minutes, or until peas are tender.
3. Strain peas through a strainer set over another medium-sized saucepan. (Stock will drain into the pot.) Remove and discard chile pepper. Mash peas through strainer into the saucepan. Add 1 cup of water to purée; set aside.
4. In a blender or food processor, purée tomato, remove to a small bowl; set aside.

Cal 49 • Fat 1.1 g

Yield: 3 Servings

Mulligatawny Soup

continued

- **½ tsp. canola oil**
- **¼ tsp. cumin seeds**
- **¼ tsp. black or yellow mustard seeds**
- **5 curry leaves**
- **2 dried red chile peppers, or to taste**
- **3 garlic cloves, crushed**
- **½ tsp. salt, or to taste**
- **1 tsp. freshly ground black pepper, or to taste**
- **¾ tsp. tamarind pulp dissolved in 1 tbsp, warm water**
- **2 tsp. finely chopped fresh cilantro**

5. Coat a large nonstick saucepan with nonstick spray. Add oil and place over medium heat. When oil is hot, add cumin and mustard seeds. Cover saucepan with a splatter guard and allow seeds to pop. When seeds have finished popping (within 30 seconds), add curry leaves, dried chile and garlic. Reduce heat to medium-low; stir once.
6. Stir in tomato and salt, increase heat to medium-high, and cook about 30 seconds. Add pea mixture and increase heat to high.
7. Add black pepper and tamarind. Mix well, bring to a boil, and remove from heat. Ladlc hot soup into bowls and garnish with cilantro.

Cal 49 • Fat 1.1 g Yield: 3 Servings

Speedy Chicken Soup

Cheer up with chicken soup. Chicken meat and chicken broth both contain tryptophan, an essential amino acid the body uses to produce the feel-good neurotransmitter serotonin.

4, 14 oz. cans reduced sodium fat-free chicken broth

2 cups chicken, cooked and shredded

2 carrots, peeled and sliced (about 1 cup)

1 cup snow peas, cut diagonally into 1" pieces (about 2 oz.)

2 scallions, sliced

salt and pepper to taste (optional)

1. In a saucepan over high heat, bring broth to a boil.
2. Add chicken, carrots, snow peas and scallions; reduce heat and simmer 5 minutes more, or until carrots are tender. Season with salt and pepper to taste, if desired. Serve or freeze for later use.

Cal 171 • Fat 5 g

Yield: 4 Servings

Quick Chicken Gumbo

More like a stew than a soup, this Creole specialty gets its thickness from gumbo file powder. Made from the bark of the sassafras tree, this seasoning can be found in the supermarket spice section.

1/3 cup long-grain white OR brown rice

1 2/3 cups water

2 tsp. olive oil

1 small onion, chopped

1 small green bell pepper, chopped

2 celery stalks, chopped

2 garlic cloves, chopped

1 tsp. paprika

1 tsp. dried thyme

1/4 tsp. salt

2, 14 1/2 oz. cans fat-free reduced-sodium chicken broth

2 cups shredded, cooked, boneless, skinless chicken breast

8 oz. can tomato sauce

1 tbsp. gumbo filé powder

1. In a small saucepan, combine rice and 2/3 cup of water. Cover and bring to a boil. Reduce heat to low. Cook, stirring often, for 7 minutes. Remove from heat and allow to sit covered.
2. Warm oil in a Dutch oven over medium heat. Add onion, pepper, celery, garlic, paprika, thyme and salt. Cook, stirring often, 5 to 7 minutes, or until vegetables are soft.
3. Add broth, chicken, tomato sauce and remaining 1 cup of water. Stir well. Cook, stirring occasionally, for 15 minutes, to blend the flavors. Remove from heat and stir in filé powder.
4. To serve, spoon gumbo into shallow bowls. Top with a dollop of rice.

Cal 138 • Fat 3 g

Yield: 8 Servings

Spicy Beef & Lentil Stew

Two tablespoons of minced fresh hot chile pepper will make this one-pot dish spicy. If you feel the diners who will be sharing this hearty stew with you may lack fortitude, use the smaller amount of chile pepper suggested.

2,14½ oz. cans no-salt added stewed tomatoes

3 cups water

8 oz. well-trimmed beef bottom round, diced

8 oz. lentils, rinsed and picked over

1 large sweet potato (12 oz.) peeled and cut into ½" cubes

1 medium onion, cut into wedges

1 to 2 tbsp. minced fresh red or green chile peppers, to taste

2 tsp. thyme

½ tsp. salt

¼ tsp. freshly ground black pepper

3 bay leaves

1. In a large saucepan, combine stewed tomatoes, water, beef, lentils, sweet potato, onion, half the chile peppers, the thyme, salt, black pepper and bay leaves. Cover and bring to a boil over medium-high heat. Reduce heat to medium-low and cook, stirring occasionally, until flavors are blended and lentils are tender, about 40 minutes.
2. With a slotted spoon, remove about 1½ cups of stew (but no meat) and purée in a blender or food processor. Return purée to stew and stir to combine. Stir in remaining chile peppers and serve. Remove and discard bay leaves.

Cal 413 • Fat 4.3 g — Yield: 4 Servings

Old-Fashioned Beef Stew

There is nothing better on a cold winter's night than a thick, hot stew.

1 tsp. Worcestershire sauce
2 bay leaves
1 garlic clove, minced
½ tsp. paprika
dash ground cloves
1½ cups water
¼ tsp. black pepper
2 cups carrots, quartered
4 medium potatoes, quartered
3 medium onions, quartered
1 tbsp. cornstarch
8 oz. lean ground beef, browned

1. Combine Worcestershire sauce, bay leaves, garlic, paprika, cloves, water and black pepper in a large soup pot.
2. Add vegetables. Cook, covered, for 30 to 40 minutes.
3. Drain vegetables, reserving liquid. Set vegetables aside and remove bay leaves.
4. Add water to reserved liquid to equal 1¼ cups. Return to soup pot.
5. Whisk cornstarch into ¼ cup cool water until smooth; pour slowly into soup pot. Heat, stirring constantly, until thickened.
6. Add meat and vegetables to soup pot. Heat and serve.

SOUPS

Cal 145 • Fat 3 g

Yield: 8 Servings

Braised Beef Stew

A hearty stew in half an hour? Now you're cooking! This 5-ingredient wonder makes a healthy meal that is bubbling over with delicious flavor – serve it now or freeze and enjoy it 2 months from now. Tomato paste may help prevent breast cancer. With 3 times more lycopene than fresh tomatoes, tomato paste is a great source of this antioxidant, which helps reduce the risk of breast cancer.

½ lb. cooked London broil (flank steak, sirloin tip or top round), cut into chunks

3 tbsp. tomato paste

1 tbsp. olive oil

14 oz. can low-sodium beef broth

1 lb. frozen mixed vegetables

1. In a skillet over high heat, heat oil and add beef and tomato paste. Cook and stir 5 minutes, or until browned.
2. Add beef broth; simmer 5 minutes. Add vegetables; simmer 15 minutes more, or until tender.

Cal 276 • Fat 10 g

Yield: 4 Servings

201 MORE Fat•Burning RECIPES
VEGETARIAN

Vegetarian Pizza

This cold appetizer pizza has a new twist – a cream cheese layer topped with lots of colorful vegetables that add fiber and vitamins.

1 pkg. (8) refrigerated buttermilk biscuits

4 oz. pkg. reduced-fat cream cheese (Neufchâtel), softened

¼ cup reduced-calorie OR nonfat mayonnaise dressing OR salad dressing

½ tsp. dried dillweed

⅛ tsp. onion powder

⅛ tsp. garlic powder

¾ cup chopped fresh spinach

½, 7 oz. jar roasted red sweet peppers, drained and chopped OR diced pimento (about ⅓ cup), drained

2 cups fresh vegetables: try broccoli florets, sliced carrots, jicama strips, sliced green onions, green sweet pepper strips, sliced and quartered yellow summer squash OR zucchini and/or cauliflower florets

1. Spray a 12" pizza pan with nonstick spray.
2. For crust, place 7 biscuits in the pan, near the edge, forming a circle. Place 1 biscuit in the center. Using fingers, press biscuits into pan to form a single crust. Bake at 375° for 12 to 15 minutes, or until light brown. Cool in pan.
2. Meanwhile, in a medium mixing bowl, stir together cream cheese, mayonnaise, dillweed, onion and garlic powders. Add spinach and roasted peppers, stirring just till combined.
3. Spread cream cheese mixture over cooled crust. Arrange vegetables over cream cheese mixture. To serve, cut into wedges. Serve immediately. Or, cover and chill for up to 24 hours.

Cal 105 • Fat 5 g

Yield: 12 Servings

Shiitake Mushrooms with Radicchio

Shiitake mushrooms and radicchio are cooked with sun-dried tomatoes and balsamic vinegar.

4 sun-dried tomatoes

1 cup water

¼ cup low-sodium tomato juice

2 garlic cloves, minced

½ medium onion, chopped

1 cup coarsely chopped shiitake mushrooms

4 cups shredded radicchio

3 tbsp. balsamic vinegar

¼ tsp. ground black pepper

1. Soak tomatoes in water for 30 minutes. Drain and chop.
2. Heat tomato juice in a large skillet. Add garlic, onion and sun-dried tomatoes and sauté until onion begins to soften, about 4 minutes.
3. Add mushrooms, radicchio and vinegar and sauté for 8 minutes more. Remove from heat, sprinkle with black pepper and serve.

Cal 124 • Fat 0 g

Yield: 4 Servings

Lemon-Garlic Kale

Kale and onion are cooked in lemon juice and garlic. Look for small bunches of rich green kale without any yellowing leaves. Kale is very rich in calcium.

2 tbsp. low-sodium nonfat chicken broth

1 medium onion, chopped

2 garlic cloves, minced

6 cups chopped kale (stems removed and discarded)

3 tbsp. lemon juice

black pepper

1. Heat broth in a large skillet. Add onion and garlic; sauté 2 minutes. Add kale and lemon juice; reduce heat to low and cook until kale is tender, about 8 minutes.
2. Drain off excess liquid; sprinkle with black pepper and serve.

Cal 41 • Fat 0 g Yield: 4 Servings

Broccolini Sauté

Also called baby broccoli, peppery broccolini is a cross between Chinese kale and broccoli.

1½ lbs. broccolini, cut into 3" pieces

6 garlic cloves, sliced

2 tbsp. pine nuts

1 tbsp. butter

2 cups cherry tomatoes, halved

salt and pepper to taste

1. In a saucepan over high heat, cook broccolini in salted boiling water 3 minutes, or until tendercrisp; drain.
2. In a skillet over medium heat, cook garlic and pine nuts in hot butter, stirring, 3 to 4 minutes, or until golden. Stir in tomatoes and cook, stirring, 2 minutes more. Add broccolini; season with salt and pepper; toss to coat.

Cal 99 • Fat 4 g Yield: 6 Servings

Parmesan Broccoli with Cherry Tomatoes

6 cups broccoli florets
16 cherry tomatoes, halved
3 tbsp. grated fresh Parmesan cheese
2 tsp. chopped fresh thyme
½ tsp. salt
½ tsp. freshly ground pepper

1. Steam broccoli florets, covered, 6 minutes, or until tendercrisp; transfer to a large bowl. Add remaining ingredients; toss gently to combine.

Cal 25 • Fat 0.8 g — Yield: 12 Servings

Green Beans in Apricot Sauce

Carrots protect your heart thanks to their rich stores of pectin, a soluble fiber. Just 2½ carrots daily can reduce blood cholesterol levels by 11%.

1 lb. green beans
3 carrots, sliced
½ cup apricot preserves, melted
1 tsp. freshly grated nutmeg
½ tsp. salt

1. In a saucepan over high heat, bring 2" water to a boil. Add green beans and carrots; cover and cook 5 minutes, or until tendercrisp. Drain; place in a serving bowl. Toss with remaining ingredients.

Cal 113 • Fat 0 g — Yield: 6 Servings

Spiced Beans & Potatoes

1 head garlic, separated into cloves but not peeled

3 tbsp. olive oil, divided

1 lb. green beans

1 lb. small red potatoes, quartered

1 red pepper, in thin strips

¼ tsp. crushed red pepper flakes

1 tsp. salt

1. Toss garlic cloves with 1 tbsp. oil. Wrap in foil. Bake at 400°F 20 minutes. Cool; Peel.
2. In a skillet, bring 1" salted water to a boil. Add beans; cook 8 minutes, or until tender. Remove; return water to a boil. Add potatoes; cook 15 minutes, or until tender; drain.
3. In a skillet over medium heat, cook red pepper, pepper flakes and garlic in remaining oil for 5 minutes. Add beans, potatoes and salt; heat through.

Cal 119 • Fat 5 g

Yield: 8 Servings

Garlic-Roasted Potatoes

Potatoes, in moderation, keep you healthy. The skins are rich in potassium, which ensures the efficient delivery of most nutrients to the cells.

2 lbs. small red potatoes, halved

6 cloves garlic, sliced

¼ cup whole parsley leaves

1 tbsp. olive oil

½ tsp. grated lemon zest

salt and pepper to taste

1. Heat oven to 425°F.
2. In a bowl, combine all ingredients; season with salt and pepper and toss to coat. Place in a roasting pan.
3. Roast 25 minutes, turning occasionally, until tender.

Cal 135 • Fat 2 g

Yield: 6 Servings

Garlic-Mashed Yukon Gold Potatoes

4 medium (about 1 lb.) Yukon gold potatoes, peeled

½ tsp. salt

6 large garlic cloves, peeled

2 tbsp. extra-virgin olive oil

salt and pepper to taste

1. Place potatoes and 5 garlic cloves in a large saucepan. Add water to cover and salt; bring to a boil over high heat. Lower heat to medium, cover partially, and cook until potatoes are tender when pierced with a knife, about 30 minutes.
2. Meanwhile, heat 1 tbsp. oil in a small nonstick skillet. Cut remaining garlic clove into paper-thin slices; add to skillet. Cook over low heat until soft but not brown, about 5 minutes; set aside.
3. When potatoes and garlic are done, drain in a colander, saving ½ cup of cooking water. Place potatoes and garlic in a large bowl, mash thoroughly with a potato masher. Add remaining oil and sautéed garlic with its oil. Add reserved cooking water a bit at a time (you may need less than ½ cup), mixing constantly, until potato mixture is smooth. Season to taste with salt and pepper.

Cal 155 • Fat 7 g

Yield: 4 Servings

Peppered Eggplant Parmigiana

Choose an eggplant that is heavy for its size, with a firm smooth skin; use within 1 to 2 days. The skin of young eggplants is edible, but older eggplants should be peeled.

2 large eggs, beaten

½ tsp. ground black pepper

¼ tsp. garlic salt

1 large eggplant, sliced into ¼" thick pieces

1 cup Italian bread crumbs

2 tbsp. olive oil

1¾ cups marinara sauce

¼ tsp. crushed red-pepper flakes, or to taste

13 oz. jar roasted sweet red peppers, drained

2 cups shredded reduced-fat mozzarella cheese

¼ cup grated Parmesan cheese

1. Preheat oven to 325°F.
2. Combine eggs, black pepper and garlic salt. Dip eggplant slices in egg mixture, then into bread crumbs.
3. Heat oil in a large nonstick skillet over medium-high heat. Coat eggplant slices with nonstick spray. In batches, quickly brown the eggplant.
4. Spread ¼ cup of sauce in a 9 x 13" baking dish. Top with eggplant slices, remaining sauce, red pepper flakes, and red peppers. Sprinkle with cheeses.
5. Bake for 40 minutes, or until cooked through and cheese is browned.

Cal 264 • Fat 12 g

Yield: 8 Servings

Ratatouille

Asparagus makes this an unusual vegetable side dish. If fresh asparagus is unavailable, substitute with fresh green beans. In summertime, Ratatouille makes a delicious cold side dish. Chill in refrigerator, then drain off any excess liquid.

2 tbsp. vegetable oil
2 cups sliced mushrooms
1 medium red onion, sliced
1 garlic clove, chopped
1 sweet green pepper, sliced
1 small eggplant (about ½ lb.), unpeeled and cut in ½" cubes
½ lb. fresh asparagus, cut in 1" lengths
1 tbsp. chopped fresh parsley
1 tbsp. chopped fresh basil or 1 tsp. dried
1 tsp. salt
¼ tsp. freshly ground pepper
2 cups cherry tomatoes, halved

1. In a large skillet or wok, heat 1 tbsp. of oil over medium-high heat; stir-fry mushrooms, onion, garlic and green pepper for 3 to 4 minutes, or until softened. With a slotted spoon, remove vegetables to a bowl and set aside.
2. Heat remaining oil in skillet. Add eggplant and asparagus; stir-fry just until tender, 3 to 4 minutes. Return mushroom mixture to pan; sprinkle with parsley, basil, salt and pepper and stir well. Add tomatoes; cover and simmer for 3 minutes. Serve immediately.

Cal 79 • Fat 4.8 g

Yield: 6 Servings

Oven-Roasted Vegetables

This is an excellent vegetable accompaniment to almost any dinner entrée! Fennel adds flavor and texture to this delicious mix of vegetables. If cooking vegetables for every meal seems a real chore, recipes such as these roasted vegetables are the perfect solution. Refrigerate leftovers and eat them the following day, or freeze them in serving-sized portions.

2 large carrots, peeled and sliced diagonally ¼" thick

2 onions, cut into eights

1 small zucchini, cut in ½" slices

2 Roma tomatoes, quartered

1 bulb fennel, cut into ½" wedges

1 sweet potato, peeled and cut into French-fry-style pieces

1 tbsp. olive oil

½ lemon, juice of

½ tsp. salt

¼ tsp. ground black pepper

2 garlic cloves, minced

1 tbsp. chopped fresh rosemary

2 tbsp. sweet wine (optional)

1. Preheat oven to 400°F.
2. In a medium roasting pan, combine all vegetables. Add oil, lemon juice, salt, pepper, garlic, rosemary and wine, if desired. Mix well with a large spoon.
3. Roast, uncovered, for 45 minutes, stirring occasionally for even roasting.

Cal 92 • Fat 3 g Yield: 6 Servings

Baked Sweet Potatoes

This is so delicious you could use it for dessert. For a treat to have on hand, divide it into 4 individual portions and freeze them. Note – sweet potatoes are sometimes labeled as yams in grocery stores, but true yams are seldom available in North America.

4 medium sweet potatoes

½ tsp. freshly grated orange zest

dash EACH ground allspice and salt

1. Place sweet potatoes in an 8" square baking pan. Cover with foil and bake at 350°F about 1½ hours, or until tender.
2. Remove sweet potatoes from oven and cut each in half; remove skin and weigh 12 oz. of sweet potatoes into a small bowl. (Remaining sweet potatoes can be frozen in measured portions and used at a later date) Add orange zest, allspice and salt.
3. Mash with potato masher or beat with electric mixer until smooth.

Cal 92 • Fat 0.2 g

Yield: 4 Servings

Parslied Spaghetti Squash

Slim down with spaghetti squash. Not only is it lower in calories and fat than its pasta namesake but spaghetti squash is also high in fiber, which speeds digestion to help you lose weight.

1 spaghetti squash (about 1½ lbs.)

2 tbsp. fresh parsley, chopped

1 tbsp. butter

3 strips bacon, cooked and crumbled

salt and cracked pepper to taste (optional)

1. Heat oven to 350°F.
2. Cut spaghetti squash lengthwise and remove seeds. Place squash halves, cut side down, on a baking sheet coated with nonstick spray.
3. Bake 45 minutes, or until squash is soft and flesh strings easily.
4. Using a fork, scrape pulp into strands and place in bowl. Add parsley, butter and bacon; toss gently. Season with salt and cracked pepper to taste, if desired.

Cal 95 • Fat 6 g

Yield: 4 Servings

Butternut Squash Surprise

Substitute sweet potato for squash. For a gingerbread flavor, try adding 1 tbsp. molasses and reducing maple syrup to 3 tbsp. Prepare recipe to end of Step 1 up to 2 days in advance. Can be baked early in the day and reheated.

1 lb. butternut squash, diced, peeled
⅓ cup dried bread crumbs
¼ cup light sour cream
¼ cup maple syrup
2 tsp. margarine OR butter
2 tsp. grated orange zest
¾ tsp. ground cinnamon
¼ tsp. ground ginger
3 eggs, separated
½ cup canned corn kernels, drained
pinch of salt

1. Preheat oven to 350°F. Spray an 8" square baking dish with nonstick spray.
2. In a pot of boiling water, cook squash for 8 minutes, or until tender; drain.
3. In a food processor, combine squash, bread crumbs, sour cream, maple syrup, margarine, orange zest, cinnamon, ginger and 2 egg yolks (discard third egg yolk); process until smooth. Transfer to a bowl; allow to cool. Stir in corn.
4. In a bowl, beat 3 egg whites and salt with an electric mixer until stiff peaks form. Stir ¼ egg whites into squash mixture. Gently fold remaining egg whites into squash. Pour into prepared pan. Bake in preheated oven for 25 minutes, or until set.

Cal 99 • Fat 3 g

Yield: 6 to 8 Servings

Vegetarian Lasagne

In this tasty lasagne the noodles are replaced with wide ribbons of zucchini – a beautiful and healthier variation of the traditional Italian version.

2 medium zucchini, 5 to 6 oz. each, sliced lengthwise into 1/4" thick slices

1 1/3 cups part-skim ricotta cheese

1/2 cup cooked, drained, chopped spinach

1 tbsp. minced fresh parsley

2 tsp. grated Parmesan cheese

1 tsp. salt

dash pepper

1 cup cooked cauliflower, puréed

1 cup sliced mushrooms

4 oz. part-skim Mozzarella cheese, sliced

1/2 cup crushed canned plum tomatoes

1/2 tsp. garlic powder

1. Place zucchini on a nonstick baking sheet. Bake at 400°F, turning once, until lightly browned, about 20 minutes.
2. In a small bowl, combine ricotta, spinach, parsley, Parmesan cheese, salt and pepper. Set aside.
3. Spray a shallow 1 1/2-quart casserole with nonstick spray; line bottom with zucchini, covering entire surface. Add ricotta mixture and spread evenly. Layer cauliflower, mushrooms, Mozzarella cheese and tomatoes over ricotta mixture; sprinkle with garlic powder.
4. Bake at 375°F until cheese melts, about 40 minutes. Remove and let set before cutting.

Cal 236 • Fat 12 g

Yield: 4 Servings

Herbed Confetti Rice

Vegetable broth, white wine and lemon zest, plus a rainbow palette of peppers combine to create an outstanding side or main dish.

2 tbsp. butter
1 large yellow onion, chopped
1 green bell pepper, chopped
1 red bell pepper, chopped
1 yellow bell pepper, chopped
2 garlic cloves, minced
1 cup long-grain white rice
14½ oz. can vegetable broth
¼ cup dry white wine
1 tsp. freshly grated lemon zest
⅛ tsp. cracked black pepper

1. In a saucepan, melt butter. Add onion and peppers and cook, stirring, 3 minutes, or until vegetables are crisp-tender. Add garlic; cook, stirring, until garlic is golden and onions are translucent.
2. Add rice; cook, stirring, 3 minutes, or until grains are well coated and slightly translucent. Do not brown rice. Add broth and wine; bring to a boil. Reduce heat to low, cover and simmer 20 minutes, or until rice is tender and liquid is absorbed. Stir in zest and pepper.

Cal 263 • Fat 7 g

Yield: 4 Servings

Sweet Red Pepper Rice

The addition of red bell peppers, red pepper flakes and paprika not only add interest to this side dish, they add vitamin C as well.

2 tsp. olive oil
1 large onion, minced
3 garlic cloves, minced
1 tsp. paprika
¼ tsp. crushed red pepper flakes
2 large red bell peppers, finely diced
1 cup long-grain rice
2 cups water
¾ tsp. grated orange zest
½ tsp. salt
¼ cup finely chopped cilantro
2 tbsp. pineapple juice

1. In a large saucepan, warm oil over low heat. Add onion and cook, stirring frequently, until onion has softened, about 7 minutes. Add garlic, paprika and red pepper flakes; stir to coat.
2. Stir in bell peppers and cook, stirring frequently, until peppers have softened, about 5 minutes.
3. Add rice and stir to coat. Add water, orange zest and salt. Bring to a boil, reduce to a simmer, cover and cook until the rice is tender and creamy, about 17 minutes.
4. Stir in cilantro and cook until heated through, about 1 minute. Remove from heat; stir in pineapple juice and serve.

Pictured on page 151.

Cal 233 • Fat 2.8 g

Yield: 4 Servings

Jeweled Jade Rice

Pick a pepper; prevent cancer. Peppers of all hues are excellent sources of beta-carotene, a powerful antioxidant that studies show may reduce the risk of stomach cancer.

5 green tea bags

3½ cups boiling water

1 tbsp. vegetable oil

1 EACH small red and yellow pepper, diced (about 1 cup)

2 carrots, peeled and grated (about ½ cup)

1½ cups long-grain rice

salt and pepper to taste (optional)

1. In a saucepan, steep green tea bags in boiling water for 5 minutes. Discard tea bags.
2. Meanwhile, in a saucepan over medium heat, heat oil and cook peppers and carrots for 3 minutes, or until tender. Add green tea, rice and salt and pepper to taste, if desired. Bring to a boil. Reduce heat and simmer 20 minutes, or until rice is tender and fluffy.

Cal 199 • Fat 3 g

Yield: 6 Servings

Kasha Pilaf

Cook a batch of kasha and divide it among portion-size plastic containers suitable for the freezer. Reheat in the microwave as a side dish, or add it to soups, stews and casseroles.

1 tbsp. olive oil

½ orange bell pepper, thinly sliced

½ red bell pepper, thinly sliced

1 carrot, thinly sliced

1 small onion, thinly sliced

½ lb. mushrooms, sliced

1 cup kasha

1 egg white, beaten

2 cups mushroom OR vegetable broth

¼ cup toasted chopped pecans

1. In a large skillet over medium heat, heat oil. Add peppers, carrot, onion and mushrooms. Cook for 5 minutes, stirring occasionally, until vegetables are tender. Remove vegetables to a bowl.
2. Mix kasha and egg white in a bowl. Add kasha mixture to skillet. Cook over medium heat, stirring to break up large clumps, for 2 to 3 minutes, separating the grains and coating them with egg.
3. Gradually stir in broth. Bring to a boil. Cover, reduce heat to a simmer, and cook for 12 to 14 minutes, or until liquid is absorbed.
4. Stir in vegetables and pecans.

Cal 176 • Fat 6 g

Yield: 4 Servings

Barley-Pine Nut Casserole

Have this when you need a starchy side dish; it's a nice change from rice and is lower on the glycemic level – very satisfying.

1 cup pearl barley

1 tbsp. salted butter

1 medium onion, chopped

¼ cup toasted pine nuts

⅓ cup finely chopped parsley (preferably Italian), plus more for garnish

¼ cup finely chopped scallions, the white and part of the green

3 cups very hot defatted chicken broth,

salt and freshly ground black pepper to taste

1. Preheat oven to 350°F.
2. Rinse barley, drain and set aside.
3. Melt butter in a 1½-quart flameproof casserole. Add onion and cook until softened, about 2 minutes. Add barley and continue cooking, stirring constantly, until barley is well coated with butter. Stir in pine nuts, parsley, scallions, hot broth and salt and pepper to taste. Mix well and bring to a boil.
4. Cover casserole and bake in preheated oven for 1 hour and 15 minutes. Fluff with 2 forks, turn into a warm serving dish, garnish with additional chopped parsley and serve.

Cal 206 • Fat 8 g

Yield: 6 Servings

Barley Pilaf

This pilaf will stay with you a lot longer than potatoes or rice.

1 cup barley
2 tbsp. butter
1 small onion, chopped
2 stalks celery, chopped
3 cups boiling water
1 tsp. salt
1 tsp. dried thyme

1. Spread barley on a baking sheet; broil for 2 to 3 minutes, until toasted and lightly browned, stirring occasionally or bake at 375°F for 6 to 8 minutes, stirring occasionally.
2. In a large saucepan, melt butter; sauté onion and celery for 2 minutes, until softened and fragrant. Stir in barley; add boiling water, salt and thyme. Cover and simmer 45 minutes, until barley is tender.

Cal 147 • Fat 4 g — Yield: 6 Servings

Vegetable Millet Stew

Serve this thick, golden treasure with whole-grain bread.

1 cup chopped carrots
½ cup chopped onion
1 cup chopped potato
1 cup shredded cabbage
½ cup chopped celery
¼ cup chopped mushrooms
2 tbsp. chopped parsley
½ cup millet
4 cups water

1. Combine all vegetables in a nonstick or iron pot.
2. Sprinkle parsley and millet over vegetables. Add 3 to 4 cups water.
3. Bring to a boil; reduce heat. Cover and simmer for 45 to 60 minutes. Keep moist with additional water. Serve.

Cal 103 • Fat Trace — Yield: 6 Servings

Chow Chow

This mustard-flavored pickled vegetable relish was brought to America by Chinese railroad workers.

8 oz. cucumber, cut into ¾" cubes

¼ cup chopped green pepper

8 oz. baby green beans

2 medium onions, peeled and thinly sliced

1 small celery heart, cut into ½" pieces

1 small cauliflower (or ½ a large one), separated into florets

8 oz. under-ripe tomatoes, sliced

salt

spiced vinegar

1. Place all vegetables in a large bowl; sprinkle with salt. Cover and leave for 24 hours.
2. Drain vegetables and rinse in cold water. Dry thoroughly, then pack into sterilized jars. Fill jars with spiced vinegar. Seal in the usual way, making sure the jar rims are clean, and leave to mature for 2 months before using.

NOTE:

- Wash vegetables thoroughly.
- Do NOT reuse jar lids.
- Leaving headspace is important when making pickles. Some recipes call for ¼ to 1" of headspace.
- Process sealed jars in a boiling water bath for about 20 minutes – timed from when water starts to boil. Remove jars and cool. Jar lids should pop as jars cool.

Cal 125 • Fat 0 g

Yield: 12 Servings

Pickled Eggplant

3 eggplants, cut in ½ lengthwise
salt
spiced cider vinegar

1. In a large saucepan, boil eggplant in salted water for 2 minutes.
2. Drain eggplant; place in sterilized jars, and cover with cold spiced cider vinegar. Seal, see note on page 97, and store for 2 weeks before using.

Cal 180 • Fat 0 g

Yield: 4 Servings

Pickled Peppers

Bright red peppers look gorgeous on your pantry shelves and taste even better.

6 large red bell peppers
3½ cups cider vinegar
6 black peppercorns
½ tsp. salt
1 sprig EACH thyme, bay leaf and parsley
4 tbsp. vegetable oil

1. Halve and seed peppers, cut into large chunks and place in 4 sterilized jars.
2. Heat vinegar, spices and herbs in a pan; bring to a boil. Boil for 5 minutes and then strain. Divide vinegar between jars, leave to cool. Add 1 tbsp. of oil to each jar before sealing, see note on page 97.

Cal 75 • Fat 0 g

Yield: 6 Servings

201 MORE Fat•Burning RECIPES

BEANS

Four-Bean Salad with Balsamic Vinaigrette

This is a very fast and easy recipe, although the flavors are anything but simple. The longer the legumes marinate, the more they pick up "snap" from the balsamic dressing. Just about any type of legumes may be used: black-eyed peas, navy beans, pinto beans and so on. It also tastes great served on top of mixed greens.

15 oz. can kidney beans, rinsed and drained
15 oz. can Great Northern beans, rinsed and drained
15 oz. can chickpeas, rinsed and drained
1 cup fresh green beans, lightly steamed
½ cup water OR nonfat chicken broth
¼ cup red wine vinegar
3 tbsp. balsamic vinegar
3 tbsp. minced fresh parsley
3 tbsp. chopped shallots
3 tbsp. olive oil
freshly ground black pepper
salt
pinch of sugar

1. In a wide, shallow bowl, place kidney beans in an even layer. Add Great Northern beans in an even layer and cover with even layers of chickpeas and green beans. Set aside.
2. In a medium bowl, whisk together water or broth, red wine vinegar, balsamic vinegar, parsley, shallots, oil and pepper, salt and sugar to taste. Pour over beans.
3. Cover and marinate for at least 2 hours, or until ready to serve. Stir beans occasionally while marinating. Taste to adjust seasoning before serving.

Cal 239 • Fat 3.4 g — Yield: 6 Servings

Pinto Bean Salad

With their red/brown streaks or freckles on a pink background, pinto beans add color and flavor to many Mexican and Spanish dishes. Like all beans, they are rich in protein, iron, calcium, B vitamins, folic acid and phosphorus, and are an excellent source of both soluble and insoluble fiber.

12 oz. cooked pinto beans

1 medium tomato, cut into 1" pieces

¼ cup diced green bell pepper

2 tbsp. diced red onion

2 tbsp. minced fresh parsley

3 tbsp. red wine vinegar

2 tsp. vegetable oil

1 small garlic clove, minced

⅛ tsp. powdered mustard

dash EACH salt and pepper

1. In a serving bowl, combine beans, tomato, green pepper, onion and parsley.
2. Combine remaining ingredients in a small bowl; mix well.
3. Pour over bean salad and toss. Cover and chill for 4 hours. Let stand at room temperature ½ hour before serving.

Cal 192 • Fat 6 g

Yield: 2 Servings

White Bean & Tomato Salad with Roasted Garlic

Italian cooks have long understood the appetizing affinity between white beans and tomatoes. Here they are combined with fresh herbs and mellow roasted garlic for a marvelous side dish with grilled fish or poultry.

1 medium head of garlic (about 3 oz.)
1½ tsp. olive oil
¼ cup minced shallots
¾ tsp. ground sage
3 cups diced plum tomatoes
⅓ cup diced celery
⅓ cup diced red onion
3 tbsp. chopped parsley
3 tbsp. minced chives
2 tbsp. fresh lemon juice
1 tbsp. balsamic vinegar
19 oz. can white beans, rinsed and drained

1. Preheat oven to 375°F.
2. Wrap garlic in aluminum foil, place on a baking sheet and bake until the garlic is soft, about 30 minutes. When cool enough to handle, unwrap, cut off stem end and squeeze out soft garlic inside. Set aside.
3. In a small nonstick skillet, warm oil over low heat. Add shallots and cook, stirring frequently, until shallots are soft, about 3 minutes. Add sage, stirring to coat.
4. Remove from heat and transfer to a large bowl. Stir in tomatoes, celery, onion, parsley, chives, lemon juice, vinegar and roasted garlic. Add white beans and toss gently to combine.

Cal 164 • Fat 2.9 g

Yield: 4 Servings

Three Bean Gumbo

Okra is a key ingredient for any gumbo. In this recipe, black-eyed peas, corn, lima beans and green beans are combined with the okra.

3¼ cups low-sodium nonfat chicken broth

2 tbsp. all-purpose flour

1 cup chopped onion

1 cup chopped celery

1 jalapeño pepper, seeded and minced

2 cups chopped green bell peppers

2 cups thinly sliced okra

1 tsp. dried oregano

1 tsp. paprika

½ tsp. dried thyme

3 cups water

2 medium tomatoes, seeded and crushed

1½ cups low-sodium black-eyed peas, rinsed, drained

1½ cups fresh or frozen, thawed lima beans

1½ cups fresh or frozen corn kernels

1 cup green beans, cut into 2" pieces

1. Heat ¼ cup broth in a large saucepan. Stir in flour. Add onion, celery, jalapeño pepper, green bell peppers, okra, oregano, paprika and thyme. Sauté for 5 minutes.
2. Add remaining broth, water and tomatoes. Bring to a boil, reduce heat and simmer for 15 minutes. Add black-eyed peas and lima beans. Simmer for 15 additional minutes.
3. Stir in corn and green beans and cook for 10 minutes more. Serve at once.

Cal 137 • Fat 1 g

Yield: 10 Servings

Lentil Surprise Stew

A mere half cup of cooked lentils has 9 grams of protein, 4 grams of fiber, and zero fat. How's that for nutritious?

1 cup dry lentils
1 tbsp. cooking oil
2 garlic cloves, minced
1 medium onion, chopped (½ cup)
4 cups water
7½ oz. can tomatoes, cut up
2 tsp. instant vegetable OR chicken bouillon granules
1 tbsp. Worcestershire sauce
½ tsp. dried thyme, crushed
¼ tsp. fennel seed, crushed
¼ tsp. pepper
1 bay leaf
2 medium carrots, chopped (1 cup)
10 oz. package frozen chopped spinach
1 tbsp. balsamic vinegar OR red wine vinegar

1. Rinse lentils; set aside.
2. In a large saucepan or Dutch oven, heat oil; cook garlic and onion until tender but not brown. Stir in lentils, water, undrained tomatoes, bouillon granules, Worcestershire sauce, thyme, fennel seed, pepper and bay leaf. Bring to a boil; reduce heat. Cover and simmer for 20 minutes.
3. Add carrots and frozen spinach. Bring to a boil, breaking up spinach with a fork; reduce heat. Cover and simmer about 15 minutes more, or until lentils are tender. Stir in vinegar. Discard bay leaf.

Cal 248 • Fat 4 g

Yield: 4 Servings

Tex-Mex Chile with Dumplings

For a family-style, meatless dinner, dish up steaming bowls of this saucy chile topped with fluffy cornmeal dumplings. Add a tossed salad to complete the meal.

1/3 cup all-purpose flour
1/3 cup yellow cornmeal
1 tsp. baking powder
1/4 tsp. salt
1 beaten egg white
1/4 cup skim milk
2 tbsp. vegetable oil
1 cup chopped onion
1 garlic clove, minced
1/4 cup water
15 oz. can garbanzo beans, rinsed and drained
15 oz. can reduced-sodium red kidney beans, rinsed and drained
2, 8 oz cans low-sodium tomato sauce
4 1/2 oz. can diced green chile peppers
2 tsp. chile powder
1 1/2 tsp. cornstarch
reduced-fat Cheddar cheese (optional)

1. In a medium bowl, stir together flour, cornmeal, baking powder and salt. In a small bowl, combine egg white, milk and oil.
2. In a skillet, combine onion, garlic and water. Bring to a boil; reduce heat. Simmer covered, about 5 minutes, or until tender. Stir in beans, tomato sauce, chile peppers and chile powder. In a small bowl stir together cornstarch and 1 tbsp. cold water. Stir into bean mixture. Cook and stir until slightly thickened. Reduce heat.
3. For dumplings, add milk mixture to cornmeal mixture; stir just until combined. Drop batter from a tbsp. on top of bubbling bean mixture, making 5 mounds. Simmer, covered, for 10 to 12 minutes, or until a toothpick inserted into the center of a dumpling comes out clean. (Do not lift cover while simmering) If desired, sprinkle with cheese.

Cal 306 • Fat 8 g

Yield: 5 Servings

Best Tandoori-Spiced Chile

Dig into my favorite protein-rich, high-fiber Tandoori-Spiced Chile with delicious complex flavors.

2 lbs. ground chicken OR turkey
1 cup bottled Tandoori Curry paste OR Tandoori Maslala paste
4 tsp. EACH curry powder and chile powder
1 tbsp. ground ginger
½ tsp. cinnamon
2 red bell peppers
2 medium-sized zucchini
2, 28 oz. cans diced tomatoes
1 leek
19 oz. can chickpeas, drained
19 oz. can lentils, drained
19 oz. can red kidney beans
½ cup chopped fresh basil

1. Lightly coat a nonstick frying pan with nonstick spray; fry chicken. Add Tandoori paste, curry, chile powder, ginger and cinnamon. Stir often with a fork, 4 to 5 minutes, to keep chicken crumbly.
2. Meanwhile, core and seed peppers and slice into 1" pieces. Slice zucchini in half lengthwise then slice each half into thick pieces. Add, with tomatoes, to chile mixture. Bring to a boil, stirring often.
3. Reduce heat to medium and partially cover with lid. Simmer, stirring occasionally. Wash and chop leek. Add chickpeas, lentils and kidney beans to chile mixture and bring to a boil. Reduce heat to medium and partially cover. Simmer for 8 to 10 minutes, stirring occasionally, until zucchini is tender. Remove from heat and stir in fresh basil.

Cal 200 • Fat 6 g   Yield: 14 servings (16 cups)

Turkey Chile

Make this chile mild or fiery – just the way you like it – by adjusting the amounts of chile powder and crushed red pepper. It can be baked in the oven or simmered on top of the stove.

6 oz. skinless turkey breast, top round beef, OR lean pork, all visible fat removed, coarsely ground

1 large onion, coarsely chopped

2 garlic cloves, chopped

1 green bell pepper, cut into 1" pieces

1 carrot, finely shredded

6 oz. can tomato paste

2 cups plus 1-quart water

15 oz. can whole or diced tomatoes

15 oz. can dark kidney beans, drained

2 to 4 tbsp. chile powder

1 tsp. cumin

salt to taste (optional)

several shakes crushed red pepper (optional; for heat)

1. If baking, preheat oven to 350°F.
2. Lightly coat a large nonstick skillet with nonstick spray. Place meat, onion and garlic in the skillet, spray lightly and sauté over medium heat, stirring, for about 5 minutes, browning meat. Do not scorch garlic. Add green pepper and carrot; stir and turn down heat to medium-low.
3. In a large soup pot (or casserole, if baking), whisk tomato paste with 2 cups water. Add meat mixture, tomatoes, kidney beans, chile powder, cumin, salt (if desired), and 1 quart water. If baking, cover and bake for 40 minutes. If cooking on the stove top, bring the mixture to a boil; stir and lower heat to simmer. Cover and simmer for 40 minutes. Add crushed red pepper if desired.

Cal 152 • Fat 1.5 g

Yield: 6 Servings

Chunky Chile

To give the baked tortilla strips a decorative edge, cut the tortillas before baking with a pasta or pastry wheel.

12 oz. beef top-round steak, all visible fat removed

2 corn tortillas

½ cup chopped onion

1 garlic clove, minced

15 oz. can kidney beans, drained and rinsed

14 oz. can stewed tomatoes with juice

2 cups water

14½ oz. can diced green chile peppers

1½ tsp. snipped fresh basil OR ½ tsp. dried basil, crushed

1 tsp. chile powder

1 tsp. instant beef bouillon granules

¼ tsp. ground cumin

¼ tsp. black pepper

¼ cup shredded reduced-fat Cheddar cheese (1 oz.)

1. Partially freeze meat, about 30 minutes. Thinly slice across the grain into bite-sized strips.
2. Cut or tear tortillas into bite-sized strips. Spread on an ungreased baking sheet. Bake at 350°F about 10 minutes, or until crisp and dry. Set aside.
3. Spray an unheated large skillet with nonstick coating. Preheat over medium-high heat. Add meat, onion and garlic. Cook and stir until meat is browned and onion is tender. Stir in kidney beans, undrained tomatoes, water, chile peppers, basil, chile powder, bouillon granules, cumin and black pepper. Bring to a boil; reduce heat. Simmer, covered, for 30 minutes, or until meat is tender.
4. Ladle into individual serving bowls. Sprinkle each serving with some of the tortilla strips and 1 tbsp. shredded cheese.

Cal 296 • Fat 7 g

Yield: 4 Servings

Linguine with Lentils

Lentils and Swiss chard, flavored in a spicy broth, combine with linguine and creamy Neufchâtel cheese for a satisfying main dish.

3 vegetable bouillon cubes dissolved in 3 cups boiling water

1 cup lentils, rinsed and drained

1 tsp. cumin seeds

2 tbsp. olive oil

1 lb. Swiss chard, rinse well, discard coarse stems, cut stems and leaves crosswise into 1/4" strips (keep stems and leaves separate)

1 large onion, chopped

2 garlic cloves, minced or pressed

1/2 tsp. crushed red pepper flakes

12 oz. dry linguine

6 oz. Neufchâtel cheese, diced

salt and pepper to taste

1. In a 6-quart pan, bring 2 cups bouillon to a boil over high heat. Add lentils and cumin. Reduce heat, cover and simmer until lentils are tender, about 30 minutes. Drain if necessary; then pour into a bowl.
2. To lentils, add oil, chard stems, onion, garlic and red pepper flakes. Cook over medium heat, stirring often, until onion is lightly browned, about 15 minutes. Add chard leaves; cook, stirring, until limp, about 3 minutes. Add lentils and remaining bouillon; cook, uncovered, until hot, about 3 minutes.
3. In a 6-quart pan, cook linguine in 3 quarts boiling water just until tender, about 7 minutes. Drain and pour into a wide bowl. Add lentil mixture and cheese, toss lightly. Season with salt and pepper.

Cal 462 • Fat 13 g

Yield: 6 Servings

Fast Bean Burritos

Hominy is made from dried yellow or white corn. It can also be served as a side dish on its own.

1⅓ cups long-grain rice
1 tsp. olive oil
½ cup chopped onion
1 tbsp. minced garlic
12 oz. can fat-free refried beans OR see recipe page 107
12 oz. can white hominy
8 flour OR corn tortillas
½ cup shredded sharp Cheddar cheese
1½ cups salsa
jalapeño peppers, chopped (optional)

1. Prepare rice according to package directions, omitting any added fat or salt.
2. Heat oil in a large nonstick skillet and sauté onion until translucent. Add garlic and sauté 1 minute more. Stir in beans and hominy and cook until hot.
3. Divide filling among tortillas; sprinkle with cheese and wrap.
4. Serve accompanied by salsa, rice and jalapeño peppers, if desired.

Cal 316 • Fat 7.8 g

Yield: 8 Servings

Refried Beans

Our version of this Mexican favorite is made typically spicy by the addition of chile powder and cumin.

2 tsp. vegetable oil
½ cup chopped onion
1 garlic clove, minced
6 oz. drained canned kidney beans
2 tbsp. tomato paste
2 tsp. chile powder
⅛ tsp. ground cumin
dash salt
2 oz. grated Cheddar cheese

1. Heat oil in a small skillet; add onion and garlic and sauté until tender. Add kidney beans, tomato paste, chile powder, cumin and salt; cook, stirring often, for 5 minutes.
2. Spray a small casserole with nonstick spray and add bean mixture. Top with Cheddar cheese and bake at 350°F for 10 to 15 minutes, or until cheese has melted.

Cal 266 • Fat 9 g   Yield: 2 Servings

Stir-Fried Spinach with Lentils

This combination of spinach and lentils makes a pleasant side dish to accompany beef, lamb, chicken or fish.

6 cups washed, packed fresh spinach
1 tbsp. butter
1 cup cooked or canned lentils
½ tsp. salt
¼ tsp. ground ginger
freshly ground pepper
1 tbsp. toasted sesame seeds

1. In a large skillet, cook spinach over medium-high heat, in just the water clinging to leaves after washing, for 2 to 3 minutes, or just until spinach barely wilts. Drain well.
2. Add butter to skillet; stir in lentils, salt, ginger and pepper to taste. Stir-fry until heated through. Serve at once, sprinkled with sesame seeds.

Cal 121 • Fat 5.5 g Yield: 4 Servings

Curried Kidney Beans

Curry, actually the turmeric (curcumin) in curry powder, has recently been shown by researchers at UCLA to play a role in slowing the development of Alzheimer's dementia. It is a powerful antioxidant and anti-inflammatory, so sprinkle curry powder on soups, stews and many other dishes.

1 tbsp. vegetable oil
½ cup chopped onion
1 small apple, cored and diced
1 garlic clove, minced
1 tbsp. enriched flour
2 tsp. curry powder
¾ cup chicken broth
12 oz. can kidney beans, drained
dash EACH salt and pepper
2 tbsp. sliced scallions

1. Heat oil in a saucepan; add onion, apple and garlic and sauté until tender. Stir in flour and curry powder and cook over low heat, stirring constantly, for 2 minutes.
2. Stirring with a wire whisk, gradually add broth; cook, stirring constantly, until sauce thickens. Add kidney beans and cook until heated. Add salt and pepper and garnish with scallions.

Cal 283 • Fat 9 g

Yield: 2 Servings

Savory Pinto Beans

A hearty main dish that's easy on the budget.

2 tsp. vegetable oil
½ cup chopped onion
1 garlic clove, minced
1 cup canned tomatoes
1 tbsp. tomato paste
½ tsp. EACH ground cumin and ground coriander
¼ tsp. salt
⅛ tsp. ground turmeric
½ cup water
12 oz. cooked pinto beans

1. Heat oil in a saucepan; add onion and garlic and sauté until softened. Stir in tomatoes, tomato paste, cumin, coriander, salt and turmeric. Add water and bring to a boil; reduce heat and simmer 10 minutes.
2. Add beans, cover and simmer 5 minutes. Remove cover and simmer 5 minutes longer.

Cal 219 • Fat 6 g — Yield: 2 Servings

Rice & Beans with Cheese

Rely on canned beans as a convenient, low-fat protein source. Rinse and drain them before using to significantly reduce the sodium or look for low-sodium varieties.

1⅓ cups water

1 cup shredded carrot

⅔ cup long-grain rice

½ cup sliced green onions

½ tsp. instant chicken OR vegetable bouillon granules

½ tsp. ground coriander

dash hot pepper sauce

15 oz. can pinto OR navy beans, rinsed and drained

1 cup low-fat cottage cheese

8 oz. carton plain low-fat yogurt

1 tbsp. snipped fresh parsley

½ cup shredded reduced-fat Cheddar cheese (2 oz.)

carrot curls (optional)

1. In a large saucepan, combine water, shredded carrot, rice, green onions, bouillon granules, coriander and hot pepper sauce. Bring to a boil; reduce heat. Simmer, covered, about 15 minutes, or until rice is tender and water is absorbed.
2. Stir in beans, cottage cheese, yogurt and parsley. Spoon into a 2-quart baking dish. Bake, covered, at 350°F for 20 to 25 minutes, or until heated through. (If desired, spoon into individual oven-safe casseroles). Sprinkle with Cheddar cheese. Bake, uncovered, for 3 to 5 minutes more, or until cheese melts. If desired, garnish with carrot curls.

Cal 276 • Fat 4 g

Yield: 5 Servings

Tortilla Black Bean Casserole

Using low-fat dairy products makes this family favorite more healthful. Low-fat sour cream, salsa, and sliced green onion are tasty toppers, too.

2 cups chopped onion
1½ cups chopped green sweet pepper
14 oz. can tomatoes, cut up
¾ cup picante sauce
2 garlic cloves, minced
2 tsp. ground cumin
2, 15 oz. cans black beans OR red kidney beans, drained and rinsed
10, 7" corn tortillas
2 cups shredded, reduced-fat Monterey Jack cheese (8 oz.)
shredded lettuce (optional)
small fresh red chile peppers, sliced (optional)

1. In a large skillet combine onion, green pepper, undrained tomatoes, picante sauce, garlic and cumin. Bring to a boil; reduce heat. Simmer, uncovered, for 10 minutes. Stir in beans.
2. Spray a 2-quart rectangular baking dish with nonstick coating. Spread ⅓ of bean mixture in dish. Top with ½ of the tortillas, overlapping as necessary, and ½ of the cheese. Add another ⅓ of bean mixture, then remaining tortillas and bean mixture. Cover and bake at 350°F for 35 to 40 minutes, or until heated through. Sprinkle with remaining cheese. Let stand for 10 minutes.
3. If desired, place some shredded lettuce on each serving plate. Cut casserole into squares; place on lettuce. Garnish with chile peppers, if desired.

Pictured opposite.

Cal 248 • Fat 4 g — Yield: 6 to 8 servings

Tortilla Black Bean Casserole, page 116
Greek Feta Salad, page 23

Cajun Black Beans & Rice

This is a great treat for lunchtime, have it with a big salad and iced tea.

2 cups long-grain rice

1 tbsp. olive oil

⅓ cup chopped onion

1 tbsp. minced garlic

1 tsp. Cajun seasoning, or to taste

2, 14 oz. cans black beans

4 oz. shredded sharp Cheddar cheese

1. Prepare rice according to package directions, omitting any added fat or salt.
2. Heat oil in a large nonstick skillet and sauté onion until translucent. Add garlic and Cajun seasoning; sauté 1 minute more.
3. Drain most of liquid from beans and add them to onion mixture. Cook about 5 minutes, adding water as needed to keep beans from drying out. Stir in cheese and heat until bubbling. Serve beans over rice.

Cal 351 • Fat 5 g

Yield: 8 Servings

Easy Four-Bean Bake

Put several kinds of canned beans in a pot and, with a few good but simple additions, you have this delicious, easy, and very pretty dish, which takes little time. Pancetta or Italian bacon adds a slightly different flavor, but, as with any bacon, you have to cut off every bit of fat with scissors. Why eat fat when the meat contains just as much flavor? Vegetables sautéed with nonstick vegetable oil spray get a rich caramelized flavor. This dish is also good without precooking the vegetables, and I do it that way when pinched for time.

2 slices thick center-cut bacon (about 2 oz.), all visible fat removed

3 celery stalks, chopped

1 medium onion, chopped

2 garlic cloves, minced

16 oz. can fat-free vegetarian baked beans in tomato sauce

2, 19 oz. cans white kidney beans (cannellini), rinsed and drained

2, 10½ oz. cans dark kidney beans, rinsed and drained

8 oz. can tomato sauce

4 tsp. dry mustard

2 tbsp. brown sugar

2 tbsp. cider OR white wine vinegar

½ tsp. hot pepper sauce

1. Coat a large nonstick skillet with nonstick spray and place over medium-high heat. Add bacon, celery, onion and garlic and cook, stirring occasionally, for 7 to 8 minutes, or until vegetables soften.
2. Add baked beans, white kidney beans, dark kidney beans, tomato sauce, dry mustard, brown sugar, vinegar and hot pepper sauce; toss to combine.
3. Lightly coat a 3-quart casserole with nonstick spray. Pour in bean mixture and bake at 400°F for 45 minutes, until hot and bubbly.

Cal 253 • Fat 1.5 g

Yield: 8 Servings

Deluxe Baked Beans

This is one of the best baked bean recipes ever! Enjoy!

1 large yellow onion, chopped

5 strips low-fat turkey bacon, diced

2, 16 oz. cans (or a 32 oz. can) vegetarian baked beans (I prefer Bush's Best vegetarian baked beans with no fat)

2 to 3 tbsp. packed brown sugar (depending on your sweet tooth)

1 tbsp. prepared mustard

½ cup chile sauce (such as Heinz)

1. Preheat oven to 350°F.
2. Coat a large nonstick frying pan with nonstick spray. Add onion and bacon and cook over medium-low heat until onion is tender and bacon is crisp. Remove from heat and stir in beans, brown sugar, mustard and chile sauce.
3. Spoon into a 2-quart casserole that has been coated with nonstick cooking spray. Bake for 35 to 45 minutes, until bubbling.

Cal 211 • Fat 1.8 g

Yield: 7 Servings

New Year's Black-Eyed Peas

Traditionally eaten on New Year's Day in the Southern US for good luck, black-eyed peas are cooked with tomatoes, bell pepper and rice.

¼ cup low-sodium nonfat chicken broth

4 garlic cloves, minced

1 medium green bell pepper, cored and chopped

2 cups canned chopped low-sodium tomatoes, with juice

1 cup canned low-sodium black-eyed peas, rinsed and drained

½ cup long-grain rice

1 cup water

1 tsp. dried thyme

¼ tsp. ground black pepper

1. Heat broth in a large skillet. Add garlic and green bell pepper; sauté until pepper begins to soften, about 5 minutes.
2. Add tomatoes, black-eyed peas, rice, water, thyme and black pepper. Bring to a boil; reduce heat, cover and simmer until rice is just tender, about 15 minutes. Serve at once.

Cal 203 • Fat 1 g

Yield: 4 Servings

PASTA

PASTA

Macaroni & Cheese

We all want comfort food once in a while. This "Mac and Cheese" has half the fat of traditional recipes. Have it with a large salad. Enjoy!

1⅓ cups hot, cooked, enriched elbow macaroni

4 oz. sharp Cheddar cheese, coarsely grated, divided

¼ cup plain unflavored yogurt

1 tbsp. plus 1 tsp. reduced-calorie mayonnaise

1 tsp. Dijon-style mustard

¼ cup diced celery

2 tbsp. diced pimiento

2 tbsp. diced green bell pepper

4 green bell pepper strips

3 pimiento strips

1. In a bowl combine macaroni with ½ of the cheese; toss until cheese is melted.
2. In a small bowl combine remaining cheese with yogurt, mayonnaise and mustard; add to macaroni mixture. Add celery, pimiento and green pepper. Toss well; cool.
3. Line a 2 x 3½ x 6¼" loaf pan with foil. Pack cooled macaroni mixture firmly into pan. Cover with foil and weight with 2 small cans (e.g. tomato paste). Refrigerate overnight.
4. Remove weight and foil. With a sharp knife, loosen loaf around edges and unmold onto a serving plate. Garnish top with vegetable strips, alternating pepper and pimiento.

Cal 388 • Fat 22 g | Yield: 2 Servings

Cavatappi Pasta with Fresh Tomato-Basil Sauce

This sauce makes the most of fresh garden tomatoes – it is bursting with flavor. It is also delicious with low-fat feta cheese – just toss cubed feta with the hot pasta and add the tomato sauce. Omit the Parmesan if using feta.

2 tbsp. extra-virgin olive oil
2 garlic cloves, minced
2 lbs. vine-ripened red tomatoes
⅓ cup julienned or chopped basil leaves
1 tbsp. balsamic vinegar
½ tsp. salt
¼ tsp. crushed hot pepper flakes
8 oz. cavatappi (corkscrew, ridged spiral macaroni) OR double elbow pasta, uncooked
¼ cup grated or shaved Parmigiano-Reggiano OR Pecorino Romano cheese

1. In a large bowl, combine oil and garlic. Set a strainer over the bowl. Cut tomatoes in half crosswise; squeeze seeds and juices into strainer. Press on seeds to extract juices; discard seeds. Coarsely chop tomatoes and add to the bowl. Stir in basil, vinegar, salt and pepper flakes. Let stand at room temperature at least 20 minutes and up to 3 hours.
2. Cook pasta according to package directions.
3. Drain and immediately toss with tomato sauce. Add cheese; toss again and transfer to serving plates.

Pictured on the front cover.

Cal 345 • Fat 11 g

Yield: 4 Servings

Summertime Linguine

This fresh sauce captures the very essence of summer flavors.

4 cups red cherry and/or yellow cherry tomatoes, halved

1 small red onion, minced

¼ cup extra-virgin olive oil

¼ cup pitted, quartered Kalamata olives

2 tbsp. drained capers

1 tbsp. minced fresh thyme

½ tsp. salt

1 pkg. (16 oz.) linguine OR any long noodle pasta

3 tbsp. grated Parmesan cheese

1. In a large bowl, combine tomatoes, onion, oil, olives, capers, thyme and salt; cover and chill 2 hours.
2. Bring 4 quarts of water to a rolling boil. Add linguine or other long noodle pasta; cook according to package directions.
3. Drain pasta; place in a large serving bowl or platter. Add tomato mixture to linguine; toss gently to combine. Sprinkle with grated Parmesan cheese.

Cal 252 • Fat 9 g

Yield: 8 Servings

Rotini & Arugula Toss

Rich in iron and vitamins A and C, arugula is very popular as a salad green in Italy. It has a bitter, peppery flavor, with hints of mustard. Use within 1 to 2 days of purchasing.

3 tbsp. extra-virgin olive oil

2 garlic cloves, minced

8 oz. rotini pasta, cooked according to package directions

8 oz. arugula, trimmed

½ cup sliced sun-dried tomatoes

½ cup sliced black olives

¼ cup sliced fresh basil leaves

2 tbsp. white balsamic vinegar

¼ tsp. EACH salt and coarsely ground black pepper

4 oz. reduced-fat goat cheese, crumbled

1. In a skillet over medium-high heat, heat olive oil; add garlic and cook 1 minute.
2. Add cooked rotini pasta, arugula and sun-dried tomatoes; sauté 1 minute, or until arugula wilts. Add next 5 ingredients; stir until heated. Top with goat cheese.

Cal 365 • Fat 13 g — Yield: 4 Servings

Penne with Asparagus, Parmesan & Pecans

Asparagus and red peppers with a creamy chive/lemon sauce – this beautiful dish can be ready in under 30 minutes.

½ lb. penne pasta

1½ lbs. asparagus, cut on the diagonal into 1½" lengths

1 medium red bell pepper, diced

⅔ cup canned chicken broth diluted with ⅔ cup water, OR 1⅓ cups homemade chicken broth

1 garlic clove, minced

½ tsp. salt

¼ tsp. freshly ground black pepper

1 tsp. cornstarch blended with 1 tbsp. water

½ cup minced chives

3 tbsp. light sour cream

1 tsp. grated lemon zest

⅓ cup grated Parmesan cheese

2 tbsp. coarsely chopped toasted pecans

1. Cook penne in a large pot of boiling water until al dente, 9 to 11 minutes, or according to package directions.
2. Meanwhile, in a large skillet, combine asparagus, bell pepper, broth, garlic, salt and black pepper. Cover and cook until asparagus is tender-crisp, about 4 minutes. Uncover; increase heat to high and bring to a boil. Stir in cornstarch mixture; cook until lightly thickened, about 1 minute.
3. Drain penne and add penne to skillet along with chives, sour cream and lemon zest. Toss well. Sprinkle on Parmesan and pecans and toss again.

Cal 335 • Fat 7.3 g Yield: 4 Servings

Pasta with Broccoli

Broccoli florets, capers and red pepper flakes create a lively fresh-tasting pasta sauce.

1 lb. dried pasta (twists, penne, OR rigatoni)

1 large bunch broccoli

4 tbsp. extra-virgin olive oil

6 garlic cloves, minced

1 tsp. red pepper flakes

salt to taste

2 tbsp. capers

1 cup freshly grated Parmesan cheese (optional)

1. Bring a large pot of water to a boil to cook pasta. Add pasta to boiling water.
2. While pasta cooks. Cut ½" off broccoli stalks and cut thick stalks away from tops. Separate tops into florets. Peel fibrous outer layer of broccoli stalks and cut stalks into bite-sized chunks.
3. Heat oil in a small pan and add garlic, red pepper and salt to taste. Cook for 1 to 2 minutes, stirring, remove from heat.
4. When pasta is 2 minutes short of being al dente, add broccoli. As soon as broccoli is crunchy-tender (test a piece of stem), drain broccoli-pasta mixture in a colander, return it to the pot and add oil mixture.
5. Add capers and season with salt to taste. Serve with grated Parmesan cheese, if desired.

Cal 431 • Fat 14 g

Yield: 6 Servings

Pasta Alfredo Primavera

This creamy, basil-flavored pasta dish is full of "power" veggies.

12 oz. rotini OR other medium-sized dry pasta

16 oz. bag fresh prewashed broccoli, baby carrots and cauliflower florets, cut into bite-sized pieces (about 4 cups)

1 cup fat-free sour cream

¼ cup fat-free cream cheese, at room temperature

2 tbsp. dried basil

⅔ cup grated Parmesan cheese

1. Cook pasta per package directions. Do not add salt or oil.
2. During the last 5 minutes of cooking time, add vegetables, and cook until they are tender. Drain well in a colander.
3. Place pasta and vegetables in a large bowl.
4. Place sour cream, cream cheese and basil in a small saucepan over medium-low heat; whisk constantly until heated through but not bubbling.
5. Fold sauce into hot pasta and vegetables, then fold in Parmesan.

Cal 473 • Fat 7 g

Yield: 4 Servings

Pasta with Veggies & Walnuts

Great tasting, plus Omega 3s and Omega 6s from walnuts! They are also very high in vitamin E. Health studies indicate that walnuts can help lower cholesterol and delay hardening of the arteries.

1 lb. winter squash, such as buttercup, kabocha, OR banana, peeled, seeded and cubed

1 lb. dried pasta, such as bow ties OR shells

1 tbsp. extra-virgin olive oil

2 garlic cloves, minced

3 tbsp. fresh parsley, minced

salt and black OR red pepper to taste

2 tbsp. chopped walnuts

¼ cup grated Parmesan cheese

1. Place squash in a saucepan with a little water; cover and steam until soft. Drain and mash squash.
2. Cook pasta until al dente.
3. While pasta is cooking, heat oil in a skillet; add garlic and sauté for 30 seconds. Add mashed squash, parsley and salt and pepper to taste.
4. Toss drained pasta with squash and serve topped with chopped walnuts and grated Parmesan cheese.

Cal 361 • Fat 6 g   Yield: 6 Servings

Whole-Wheat Pasta Shells with Spicy Tomato Pesto & Winter Greens

Whole-wheat pastas have a firmer, chewier texture than white-flour pastas, and a robust flavor that stands up well to strong-flavored olive oil based sauces or pestos.

Spicy Tomato Pesto

1 cup boiling water
½ cup sun-dried tomatoes, packed without oil
¼ cup sliced almonds
¼ cup (1 oz.) grated Parmesan cheese
¼ cup chopped fresh basil
2 garlic cloves, minced
½ tsp. salt
¼ tsp. crushed red pepper
1 ½ tbsp. extra-virgin olive oil

1. **Pesto**: Combine water and tomatoes in a bowl; let stand 30 minutes, or until soft. Drain tomatoes in a colander over a bowl, reserving ½ cup liquid.
2. Drop tomatoes, almonds, cheese, basil and garlic through food chute with food processor on; process until minced. Add salt and red pepper. Slowly pour 1½ tbsp. oil through food chute; process until well blended, scraping sides. Add reserved soaking liquid, 1 tbsp. at a time, until smooth. Set aside.

Cal 355 • Fat 12.4 g

Yield: 5 Servings

Whole-Wheat Pasta Shells with Spicy Tomato Pesto & Winter Greens

Continued

Greens

1 tbsp. olive oil
1 cup chopped onion
3 cups trimmed Swiss chard, sliced into ½" strips
¼ cup water
¼ tsp. salt
¼ tsp. black pepper

Pasta

8 cups hot, cooked whole-wheat pasta shells
4 tsp. grated Parmesan cheese

3. **Greens**: Heat oil in a large nonstick skillet over medium-high heat. Add onions; cook 10 minutes, or until lightly browned, stirring frequently. Add Swiss chard; stir-fry 1 minute, or until leaves turn bright green. Add water, salt and pepper; cover and cook 2 minutes.
4. Combine pesto and pasta in a large bowl. Add greens; toss well. Sprinkle with Parmesan.

Cal 355 • Fat 12.4 g   Yield: 5 Servings

Penne with Balsamic-Roasted Vegetables

Caramelized roasted vegetables make a fabulous pasta sauce.

PASTA

2 small eggplants (about ½ lb. each), quartered lengthwise and cut into 1" cubes

2 ripe beefsteak tomatoes, cut into 1" pieces

16 baby carrots

⅓ cup plus 1 tbsp. balsamic vinegar, divided

2 tbsp. chopped fresh oregano, OR 2 tsp. dried

2 tbsp. olive oil, divided

½ tsp. salt

½ tsp. freshly ground black pepper

12 oz. uncooked penne pasta

1 cup reduced-sodium, nonfat chicken OR vegetable broth

½ cup vermouth OR dry white wine

4 tbsp. grated Parmesan cheese

1. Preheat oven to 450°F.
2. In a large bowl, combine eggplant, tomatoes, carrots, ⅓ cup balsamic vinegar, oregano, 1 tbsp. oil, salt and pepper. Toss to coat.
3. Arrange vegetables on a large baking sheet coated with nonstick spray. Roast 20 minutes, or until golden brown and tender. Remove vegetables from oven and set aside.
4. Meanwhile, cook penne in a large pot of rapidly boiling water until just tender, about 10 minutes. Drain and transfer to a large bowl.
5. Add remaining tbsp. balsamic vinegar and olive oil, chicken broth and vermouth. Toss to coat. Add roasted vegetables; toss to combine. Spoon pasta and vegetables into shallow bowls and top with grated Parmesan.

Cal 509 • Fat 10 g Yield: 4 servings

Roasted Garlic Mac & Cheese

Healthy soy appears in 3 ingredients; roasted garlic adds rich mellow flavor.

2 cups dry soy pasta (rotelli if possible)

¼ cup trans-free margarine

4 to 6 roasted garlic cloves, skins removed

3 tbsp. all-purpose flour

2 cups unflavored soy milk

2 to 3 tbsp. brown OR Dijon mustard

¼ tsp. ground white pepper

sea salt

2 cups Cheddar cheese-flavored soy shreds

2 tbsp. dried bread crumbs

¼ tsp. ground paprika

chopped black olives for garnish

1. Prepare pasta per package directions, omitting 3 to 4 minutes from cooking time if you plan to finish recipe in the oven. Drain.
2. Melt margarine in a medium saucepan; add garlic, mashing to incorporate.
3. Add flour 1 tbsp. at a time, stirring well to combine. Add milk, about ½ cup at a time, stirring continuously until thickened.
4. Add mustard, pepper, and salt to taste. Bring to a slow boil.
5. Take saucepan off heat; stir in soy shreds. Add pasta to saucepan and stir to coat.
6. Place in a lightly greased 2-quart baking dish, sprinkle with bread crumbs and paprika. Bake at 350°F for 20 to 25 minutes. Garnish with olives.

Cal 230 • Fat 8 g　　Yield: 6 Servings

Tubular Pasta

Like, the flavor of this pasta dish is sooo good. Rigatoni tubes with 4 kinds of cheese! Have with a huge salad and enjoy!

- **12 oz. uncooked rigatoni (about 7 cups dry)**
- **½ cup chopped onion**
- **2 garlic cloves, minced**
- **3 cups tomato sauce**
- **2 tbsp. reduced-sodium soy sauce**
- **2 tsp. brown sugar**
- **1 tsp. dried oregano**
- **1 tsp. dried basil**
- **½ tsp. crushed red pepper flakes**
- **¼ tsp. black pepper**
- **¾ cup low-fat (1%) cottage cheese**
- **½ cup part-skim ricotta cheese**
- **¼ cup Parmesan cheese**
- **1 egg white**
- **10 oz. package frozen spinach, thawed, squeezed dry and chopped**
- **½ cup shredded part-skim mozzarella cheese (2 oz.)**
- **1 tbsp. chopped fresh parsley (optional)**

1. Prepare rigatoni; shorten cooking time by 1 to 2 minutes – pasta should be slightly undercooked. Drain. Rinse with cold water; drain again. Set aside.
2. Spray a medium saucepan with nonstick spray. Add onions and garlic. Cook; stir over medium heat for 3 to 4 minutes. Add tomato sauce and next 6 ingredients. Bring to a boil. Reduce heat to low. Cover; simmer 5 minutes, stirring occasionally. Remove from heat.
3. Combine cheeses and egg white in a large bowl. Stir in spinach. Mix in rigatoni.
4. Spray a large casserole with nonstick spray. Spread ½ cup sauce in casserole, followed by ½ rigatoni. Pour ½ remaining sauce over rigatoni, followed by cheese. Repeat layering: rigatoni, sauce and cheese. Sprinkle with parsley. Cover; bake at 350°F for 30 minutes. Serve with additional Parmesan.

Cal 378 • Fat 7.3 g — Yield: 6 Servings

Creamy Cannellini 'n' Pasta

This creamy mushroom sauce is perfect with the mild, nutty flavor of cannellini beans.

½ cup finely chopped mushrooms

salt

2 tsp. trans-free margarine

⅛ tsp. minced fresh garlic

⅛ tsp. dried oregano

dash pepper

2 tsp. enriched flour

1 cup skim milk

6 oz. cooked cannellini beans (white kidney beans)

1⅓ cups cooked enriched spiral pasta OR elbow macaroni

1. Combine mushrooms and a dash of salt in small skillet. Cook over medium heat, stirring occasionally, until most of liquid is evaporated; set aside.
2. Melt margarine in a small saucepan. Add garlic, oregano and pepper; cook over medium heat until margarine begins to foam. Stirring constantly, add flour and cook 2 minutes. Remove from heat. Slowly pour in milk, stirring briskly with a wire whisk. Stir until margarine and flour are well blended with milk. Add ¼ tsp. salt, return to heat and slowly bring to a boil, stirring occasionally. Reduce heat to low.
3. Add mushrooms, beans and macaroni to sauce and stir to combine; cook 2 to 3 minutes, or until thoroughly heated.

Cal 271 • Fat 5 g

Yield: 2 Servings

Linguine with Red Clam Sauce

A favorite Italian wedding of ingredients, this linguine with red clam sauce calls for fresh littleneck clams in their shells. More exciting to look at than a sauce with chopped clams, you could serve this either as an entrée or in smaller portions as a first course followed by grilled fish and a summer salad. For dessert, stay in the warm-weather mode with fresh raspberries and lemon sorbet.

1 tbsp. + 1 tsp. extra-virgin olive oil

2 large red bell peppers, diced

1 medium onion, chopped

4 garlic cloves, minced

1 tsp. dried oregano

½ tsp. freshly ground black pepper

¼ tsp. crushed red pepper flakes

¼ cup dry white wine OR canned chicken broth

16 oz. can crushed tomatoes

8 oz. can no-salt added tomato sauce

½ lb. linguine

2 dozen littleneck clams, scrubbed

1. In a Dutch oven, warm oil over medium-high heat until hot but not smoking. Stir in peppers, onion, garlic, oregano, black pepper and red pepper flakes; sauté until vegetables are tender, 4 to 6 minutes.
2. Stir in wine; bring to a simmer. Stir in tomatoes and tomato sauce; bring to a boil. Reduce heat to low, cover and simmer for 15 minutes, stirring occasionally.
3. Meanwhile, cook linguine in a large pot of boiling water until al dente, 9 to 11 minutes. Drain in a colander and transfer to a large serving bowl.
4. Add clams to sauce; cover and cook, stirring frequently, until clams open, 10 to 12 minutes. (Discard any clams that do not open.) Pour sauce and clams over pasta.

Cal 377 • Fat 6.5 g

Yield: 4 Servings

Fettuccine with Mussels & Spinach

The small black tuft that protrudes from between the shell halves of a mussel is called the beard. It needs to be removed before the mussels are cooked. As you scrub the shellfish, pull the beards out with your fingers and then rinse the mussels well.

½ lb. fettuccine

½ cup dry white wine

½ tsp. dried thyme

2 dozen mussels, scrubbed and debearded

1 tbsp. extra-virgin olive oil

4 garlic cloves, thinly sliced

12 cups (loosely packed) stemmed spinach

½ tsp. freshly ground black pepper

½ tsp. salt

1. In a large pot of boiling water, cook pasta until al dente, 8 to 10 minutes. Drain in a colander.
2. In a large saucepan, combine wine and thyme. Cover; bring to a boil over high heat. Stir in mussels; reduce heat to medium-high, cover and cook, stirring until mussels open, 4 to 6 minutes. Remove pan from heat. (Discard mussels that don't open.)
3. Drain pasta, add oil and garlic to pasta. Cook over high heat, stirring constantly, until garlic is golden, 1 to 2 minutes. Add spinach, pepper and salt; cook, stirring, until spinach is just wilted, 3 to 4 minutes.
4. Add drained pasta to spinach mixture; toss until heated through. Remove from heat.
5. Reserve 4 mussels in their shells. Shell remaining mussels; add to pasta.
6. Line a fine-mesh sieve with cheesecloth; set over a small bowl. Pour mussel cooking juices through strainer; add strained juices to pasta.
7. To serve, divide pasta among 4 pasta bowls; top each with a mussel in the shell.

Cal 359 • Fat 7.7 g

Yield: 4 Servings

Seafood-Stuffed Shells

Most North American surimi (formed fish) is made from pollock, which is part of the cod family. It has a delicate flavor that is slightly sweet. Unopened surimi can be stored in the refrigerator for up to 2 months; once opened it should be used within 2 days.

1 cup grape tomatoes
1 lb. surimi (imitation crabmeat)
⅔ cup nonfat mayonnaise
½ cup celery, sliced
¼ cup chopped fresh basil
2 tbsp. toasted pine nuts
4 oz. large pasta shells, cooked according to package directions and rinsed in cold water

1. Using a sharp knife, halve tomatoes. In a large bowl, combine tomatoes, surimi, mayonnaise, celery, basil and pine nuts; toss gently to coat.
2. Fill cooked, cooled shells with surimi mixture.

Cal 189 • Fat 3 g

Yield: 6 Servings

Shells with Tomatoes, Peppers & Cod

The zesty flavors of Spain are at play in this dish of pasta shells topped with tomato sauce, fresh cod, peppers and green olives. If cod is unavailable, use scrod, haddock or another firm-fleshed white fish that has identity and that will flake easily. The texture of the fish is important here.

1 tbsp. olive oil

¾ cup finely chopped onion

3 garlic cloves, finely chopped

1 medium red bell pepper, diced

2 cups chopped tomatoes

½ tsp. grated orange zest

¼ cup orange juice

4 drops of hot pepper sauce

½ tsp. salt

½ tsp. ground ginger

½ lb. pasta shells

1¼ lbs. cod fillets, cut into 4 pieces

2½ tsp. cornstarch blended with 1½ tsp. water

8 green olives, pitted and coarsely chopped

3 tbsp. chopped flat-leaf parsley

1. In a large nonstick skillet over medium-low, heat oil. Add onion and garlic; cook, stirring until onion has softened, about 7 minutes. Add pepper; increase heat to medium; cook until pepper has softened, about 5 minutes.
2. Stir in tomatoes, orange zest, orange juice, hot pepper sauce, salt and ginger. Bring to a boil, then reduce to a simmer; cook for 5 minutes to blend flavors.
3. Cook pasta in a large pot of boiling water until al dente, 7 to 9 minutes. Drain in a colander.
4. Place cod on top of the tomato-pepper mixture, cover; cook until fish flakes when tested with a fork, 10 minutes.
5. Add cornstarch mixture to skillet, bring to a boil; cook until sauce is lightly thickened. Flake cod with a fork. Stir in olives and parsley. Toss with hot pasta and serve.

Cal 419 • Fat 6.6 g

Yield: 4 Servings

Salmon Capellini

Lemon, Dijon and dill complement the springtime flavors of asparagus and grilled salmon. Capellini, with slightly more thickness than angel hair pasta, makes this an elegant dish.

½ lb. asparagus, cut into 1" pieces
⅓ cup vegetable broth
2 tbsp. fresh lemon juice
1 tbsp. Dijon mustard
½ tsp. salt
¼ tsp. cracked black pepper
2 tbsp. chopped fresh dillweed, divided
2 tbsp. extra-virgin olive oil
8 oz. capellini pasta, cooked
1 small shallot, minced
8 oz. salmon filet, grilled, flaked

1. Blanch asparagus 2 minutes in boiling salted water; refresh in cold water.
2. Whisk together broth, lemon juice, mustard, salt, pepper and 1 tbsp. dillweed. Slowly whisk in oil.
3. Toss pasta with half the dressing, shallot and remaining dillweed; divide evenly between 4 plates. Arrange asparagus and salmon in center of each plate; drizzle with remaining dressing.

Cal 394 •Fat 14 g

Yield: 4 Servings

Wide Noodles with Curried Chicken

★★★ Delicious! ★★★

1 tbsp. olive oil
3 garlic cloves, minced
1 tsp. cumin
1 tsp. ground coriander
¾ tsp. ground ginger
¾ tsp. turmeric
½ tsp. paprika
¾ lb. sweet potatoes, peeled, cut into ½" chunks
1 large carrot, thinly sliced
¾ cup canned chicken broth diluted with ½ cup water, OR 1¼ cups homemade chicken broth
½ lb. skinless, boneless chicken breast cut into ½" chunks
¼ tsp. salt
¼ tsp. freshly ground pepper
½ lb. wide noodles
½ cup frozen peas
⅓ cup plain nonfat yogurt
1 tbsp. flour
1 tsp. peanut butter
3 tbsp. chopped cilantro

1. In a large nonstick skillet, warm oil over medium heat until hot but not smoking. Add garlic; cook until fragrant, about 1 minute. Stir in cumin, coriander, ginger, turmeric and paprika; cook for 1 minute.
2. Add sweet potatoes, carrot and ¼ cup chicken broth; cook, stirring frequently, until carrot is almost tender, about 4 minutes.
3. Stir in chicken, coating well. Add remaining broth, salt and pepper. Bring to a boil, reduce to a simmer; cook until potatoes and chicken are cooked through, about 5 minutes.
4. In a large pot of boiling water, cook noodles until al dente, 7 to 9 minutes. Add peas for the last minute or so.
5. In a small bowl, blend yogurt and flour. Whisk yogurt mixture into chicken mixture, then stir in peanut butter. Drain pasta and peas; toss with chicken mixture and cilantro.

Cal 437 • Fat 7.9 g

Yield: 4 Servings

Penne Pasta

Too good for words! The zest and zing of this pasta dish will be stored in your memory bank forever.

1 cup sun-dried tomatoes
3 cups sliced mushrooms
12 oz. uncooked penne pasta (about 4 cups dry)
4 slices raw turkey bacon, cut crosswise into ½" sections
3 garlic cloves, minced
1 cup sliced red onion rings
2 cups chopped fresh spinach
2 tbsp. chopped fresh basil OR 1 tsp. dried basil
½ tsp. crushed red pepper flakes
freshly ground black pepper to taste
2 tbsp. Parmesan cheese
2 tbsp. chopped fresh parsley

1. Pour 1 cup boiling water over sun-dried tomatoes and let soak for 5 minutes. Drain and chop. Set aside.
2. Place mushrooms in a medium bowl with ¼ cup water. Microwave on HIGH power for 5 minutes. Drain and set aside.
3. Cook penne according to package directions. Drain and keep warm.
4. Cook bacon in a large skillet over medium-high heat until crisp. Add garlic and cook for 1 minute. Do not discard drippings! Add onion, spinach, sun-dried tomatoes, mushrooms, basil and red pepper flakes. Cook and stir for 4 to 5 minutes, until onions are tender.
5. Toss bacon/vegetable mixture with hot pasta. Divide between 4 serving dishes. Top each with freshly ground black pepper and Parmesan cheese. Sprinkle with parsley. Serve immediately.

Cal 476 • Fat 8 g | Yield: 4 Servings

Sesame Penne & Pork

Sugar snap peas or sugar peas should be cooked very briefly to keep their bright colour and crisp texture.

8 oz. penne pasta
1 tbsp. sesame oil
1 lb. pork tenderloin, sliced diagonally in 1/4" slices
1 red pepper, sliced
1 red onion, sliced
3 tbsp. hoisin sauce
3 tbsp. low-sodium soy sauce
1/2 lb. sugar snap peas

1. Cook penne in salted boiling water according to package directions; drain and keep warm.
2. Meanwhile, heat sesame oil in a wok or large skillet over high heat until very hot but not smoking. Add sliced pork and cook, stirring for 3 minutes. Add red pepper, red onion, hoisin sauce, soy sauce, peas and 1/4 cup water; cook, stirring rapidly, for 5 minutes more. Serve over pasta.

Cal 466 • Fat 11 g   Yield: 4 Servings

Herbed Wonton Ravioli

Ricotta salata is a mellow, nutty, mild-flavored aged ricotta that is ideal for pasta dishes and salads.

½ cup crumbled ricotta salata cheese
½ cup light ricotta cheese
¼ cup chopped parsley
½ tsp. grated lemon zest
1 egg, separated
16 wonton wrappers, halved
2 tbsp. olive oil
½ EACH small red, yellow and green peppers, chopped
2 oz. prosciutto, sliced
2 tbsp. chopped fresh sage

1. Combine cheeses, parsley, lemon zest and egg yolk.
2. Place ½ tbsp. of cheese mixture on bottom half of each wrapper. Brush edges with egg white. Fold in half; press to seal.
3. In a large saucepan of boiling water, over high heat, boil ravioli 2 minutes; drain.
4. In a large skillet over medium heat, heat oil; add peppers, prosciutto and sage; cook for 5 minutes. Add ravioli; gently toss until heated through.

Cal 248 • Fat 11 g Yield: 4 Servings

201 MORE Fat•Burning RECIPES

SEAFOOD

POULTRY

Shrimp Creole

Creole recipes mirror the cultural heritage of New Orleans and include the best of French, Spanish and African cooking.

12 oz. fresh or frozen peeled and deveined large shrimp, rinsed

¾ cup chopped onion

¾ cup chopped red bell pepper

½ cup chopped celery

14½ oz. can Cajun-style OR Mexican-style stewed tomatoes, undrained and cut up

2 tbsp. snipped fresh thyme or 1 tsp. dried thyme, crushed

1 tsp. instant chicken bouillon granules

1 tsp. sugar

2 garlic cloves, minced

several dashes hot pepper sauce (optional)

2 tsp. cornstarch

2 cups hot cooked brown rice

¼ cup snipped fresh parsley OR celery tops

1. In a large saucepan, bring 4 cups water to a boil; add shrimp. Return to boiling; reduce heat. Simmer, uncovered, for 1 to 3 minutes, or until shrimp turns pink. Drain in colander. Set aside.
2. In same saucepan, combine onion, red pepper, celery and ⅓ cup water. Bring to a boil; reduce heat. Simmer, covered, for 3 to 4 minutes, or until vegetables are crisp-tender. Do not drain.
3. Stir in tomatoes, thyme, bouillon granules, sugar, garlic and hot pepper sauce. Simmer, covered, for 8 minutes.
4. Combine cornstarch and 1 tbsp. cold water; stir into saucepan. Cook and stir over medium heat until thickened and bubbly. Reduce heat; Cook and stir for 2 minutes more. Stir in shrimp; heat through. Combine rice and parsley. Serve Shrimp Creole with rice.

Cal 231 • Fat 1 g

Yield: 4 Servings

Stir-Fried Shrimp with Scallions

Here's a fantastic dish that takes just 10 minutes to prepare.

3 garlic cloves, crushed
½ tsp. peeled, grated ginger
12 scallions, chopped
8 oz. medium-sized cooked shrimp
¼ tsp. turmeric
¼ tsp. salt, or to taste
1 tbsp. fresh lemon juice
1 lemon, cut into wedges

1. Generously spray a large nonstick skillet with nonstick spray. Place over medium-high heat, then add garlic, ginger and scallions. Stir-fry about 2 minutes, until scallions begin to brown.
2. Add shrimp, turmeric and salt. Stir-fry for 5 minutes, until shrimp turns pink. Add lemon juice and cook another minute.
3. Transfer to a serving bowl and garnish with lemon wedges. Serve hot.

Cal 115 • Fat 1.9 g

Yield: 3 Servings

Szechwan Shrimp

Peppery Szechwan dishes are perfect for everyone who loves spicy food.

1 lb. fresh or frozen shrimp in shells

Szechwan Sauce

3 tbsp. water

2 tbsp. salsa

1 tbsp. reduced-sodium soy sauce

1 tbsp. rice wine, dry sherry OR water

2 tsp. cornstarch

1 tsp. honey

1 tsp. grated fresh ginger or ¼ tsp. ground ginger

½ tsp. crushed red pepper

1 tbsp. peanut OR vegetable oil

½ cup sliced green onions

4 garlic cloves, minced

2 cups hot cooked rice

1. Thaw shrimp, if frozen. Peel and devein shrimp; cut in half lengthwise. Rinse; pat dry with paper towels. Set aside.
2. **Sauce**: In a small mixing bowl stir together water, salsa, soy sauce, rice wine, cornstarch, honey, ground ginger (if using), and crushed red pepper. Set aside.
3. Pour oil into a large skillet or wok. Heat over medium-high heat. Add green onions, garlic, and grated fresh ginger (if using); stir-fry for 30 seconds.
4. Add shrimp. Stir-fry for 2 to 3 minutes, or until shrimp turns pink; push to side of skillet or wok. Stir sauce; add to center of skillet. Cook and stir until thickened and bubbly. Cook and stir for 2 minutes more. Serve with rice.

Pictured opposite.

Cal 232 • Fat 4 g

Yield: 4 Servings

Szechwan Shrimp, page 150
Sweet Red Pepper Rice, page 92

Pepper-Seared Sea Scallops

This elegant recipe is fast and simple to make.

20 sea scallops
1 tsp. olive oil
coarsely cracked black pepper
salt

1. Rinse scallops and pat dry between paper towels.
2. Warm oil in a large nonstick frying pan over medium-high heat.
3. Coat scallops with the pepper and salt to taste.
4. Add scallops to pan and cook for 3 to 5 minutes on each side, being careful to neither overcook nor undercook. Serve immediately.

Cal 72 • Fat 1.7 g

Yield: 4 Servings

Ginger Salmon

Fabulous flavor and a snap to make, this dish is everyday easy and company elegant. Salmon is also a nutrition powerhouse – high in protein, vitamin A, the B vitamins and Omega 3 fatty acids.

Soy Ginger Marinade

2 tbsp. rice vinegar
1 tbsp. low-sodium soy sauce
1 tsp. sesame oil
1 tsp. minced ginger
½ tsp. minced garlic

1⅛ lb. salmon fillet
2 tbsp. minced scallion
lime wedges for garnish

1. **Marinade**: Combine all ingredients in a small bowl; whisk to mix.
2. Place salmon in a shallow baking dish and pour marinade over it. Cover with plastic wrap and marinate in the refrigerator for 1 hour.
3. Preheat oven to 450°F.
4. Spray a baking sheet with nonstick spray. Place fish on baking sheet; brush with remaining marinade and cook 7 to 10 minutes, or until cooked through.
4. Sprinkle scallions over fish and garnish with lime wedges.

Cal 133 • Fat 3.7 g — Yield: 6 Servings

Poached Fish with Horseradish Sauce

Tiny boiled potatoes and slivered green onions garnish a savory supper dish that's delicious prepared with any of a variety of fish. The simple sauce, based on the poaching liquid, gets a thermogenic boost from horseradish.

1½ lbs. boneless, skinless lingcod, halibut, rockfish, sole fillets OR steaks (fillets no thicker than 1", steaks about 1" thick)

⅔ cup low-sodium chicken broth

1 tbsp. EACH cornstarch and prepared horseradish

8 to 12 hot boiled tiny potatoes (each about 1" in diameter)

3 green onions, cut into 2" lengths and slivered

1. Rinse fish and pat dry; fold any thin fillets in half. Arrange fish in a shallow 8 or 9" baking dish. Pour broth over fish. Cover and bake at 400°F until fish is just opaque but still moist in thickest part; cut to test, about 15 minutes. With a slotted spatula, lift fish to a warm platter; keep warm.
2. Drain cooking liquid from baking dish into a measuring cup; you should have about 1 cup. If necessary, boil to reduce to 1 cup or add more broth to make 1 cup. In a 1½ to 2-quart pan, blend cornstarch, horseradish and cooking liquid until smooth. Bring to a boil over high heat, stirring.
3. To serve, spoon sauce evenly over fish. Arrange potatoes on platter around fish; sprinkle with onions.

Cal 208 • Fat 2 g

Yield: 4 Servings

Halibut Supreme

Other white fish, such as sole, flounder or turbot can be substituted. Toast pecans either in 400°F oven or in skillet on stove top for about 2 minutes, or until brown.

½ cup bread crumbs
1 tsp. dried parsley
½ tsp. dried basil
½ tsp. crushed garlic
1½ tsp. grated Parmesan cheese
1 lb. halibut, cut into 4 serving-sized pieces
1 egg white, lightly beaten
2 tbsp. olive oil
2 tbsp. white wine
4 tsp. lemon juice
1 tbsp. chopped fresh parsley
1 green onion, chopped
1 tbsp. chopped toasted pecans

1. Preheat oven to 400°F.
2. In a bowl, combine bread crumbs, parsley, basil, garlic and Parmesan cheese. Dip halibut pieces into egg white, then into bread crumb mixture.
3. In a large nonstick skillet, heat 1 tbsp. oil over medium-high heat. Add fish; cook until browned on both sides.
4. Transfer fish to a baking dish; bake for 5 to 10 minutes, or until fish flakes easily with fork. Remove to a serving platter; keep warm.
5. In the skillet, heat remaining oil; add wine, lemon juice, parsley, onion and pecans; cook for 1 minute. Pour over fish. Serve immediately.

Cal 231 • Fat 9 g

Yield: 4 Servings

Garlic Fish Kabobs

Generous amounts of garlic, ginger and cayenne pepper give this magnificent skewered fish its incomparable flavor, along with a thermogenic effect that can't be beat.

1 lb. halibut, swordfish OR OTHER firm-textured fish, skinned and cut into 1 x 1½" chunks (about 16 pieces)

Ginger-Garlic Marinade

1 tsp. chopped fresh ginger

4 garlic cloves, crushed

½ tsp. cayenne pepper

2 tbsp. fresh lemon juice

¼ tsp. salt, or to taste

1 small red onion, cut into thin rings

1 tbsp. fresh lemon juice for garnish

1. Rinse fish under cold water; pat dry with paper towels.
2. **Marinade**: In a medium-sized bowl, combine all ingredients. Add fish and toss gently to coat. Cover and marinate in the refrigerator for 2 hours.
3. Skewer even amounts of marinated fish onto 4 skewers, then spray with nonstick spray. Cook on a heated barbecue grill about 10 to 12 minutes, turning and basting with reserved marinade until fish is cooked.
4. Arrange kabobs on a serving platter, top with onion rings and drizzle with lemon juice. Serve immediately.

Cal 131 • Fat 2.7 g

Yield: 4 Servings

Terrific Tuna Casserole

Carrots also make a colorful addition to this thrifty wholesome casserole and frozen mixed or other vegetables may be substituted for peas. Tuna is rich in Omega 3 fatty acids, protein, minerals and vitamins and it is low in saturated fat and cholesterol.

2, 6½ oz. cans water-packed tuna
1 cup low-fat yogurt
1 tbsp dried onion
1 celery stalk
10 oz. package frozen peas
½ tsp. garlic powder
¼ tsp. black pepper
3 cups whole-wheat noodles, cooked

1. Combine all ingredients, except noodles. Mix well and combine with noodles.
2. Place in a nonstick casserole and bake at 350°F for 30 minutes. Serve.

Cal 209 • Fat 2 g

Yield: 10 Servings

Tahitian Tuna Cakes with Ginger Dressing & Papaya Salsa

My favorite tuna cakes, they'll become yours too!

Tuna Cakes

2, 6½ oz. cans water-packed tuna, drained and flaked

½ cup liquid egg substitute

¼ cup chopped scallion

1 cup dried bread crumbs

1 tbsp. olive oil

cilantro for garnish

Ginger Dressing

1 cup fat-free plain yogurt

2 tbsp. lime juice

1 tbsp. grated fresh ginger

1 tbsp. coarse-grain mustard

2 tsp. olive oil

½ tsp. ground cumin

Papaya Salsa

1½ cups cubed papaya

½ cup chopped red bell pepper

2 tbsp. chopped fresh cilantro

1 tbsp. lime juice

1 tbsp. honey

¼ tsp. ground red pepper

1. **Tuna Cakes**: In a large bowl, combine tuna, egg substitute, scallions, ⅔ cup of bread crumbs and ¼ cup of ginger dressing. Mix well. Shape into ½" thick patties. Coat with remaining ⅓ cup bread crumbs.
2. **Ginger Dressing**: In a small bowl, whisk together all dressing ingredients. Set aside.
3. **Papaya Salsa**: In a small bowl, combine all salsa ingredients. Set aside.
4. In a large nonstick skillet over medium heat, warm 1 tbsp. oil. Add patties and sauté for 3 minutes per side, or until golden brown.
5. Transfer patties to individual plates. Drizzle with remaining ginger dressing. Serve with salsa and garnish with sprigs of cilantro.

Cal 346 • Fat 9 g

Yield: 4 Servings

Orange Chicken Stir-Fry

In this family favorite, orange juice and balsamic vinegar combine to give chicken and vegetables a delightful sweet-sour tang.

⅓ cup orange juice
¼ cup chicken stock
2 tbsp. balsamic vinegar
1 tbsp. sugar
2 tsp. grated orange zest
2 tsp. cornstarch
¼ tsp. salt
4 tsp. olive oil
1 lb. lean boneless chicken breasts, cut into strips
2 medium zucchini, halved lengthwise and sliced
1 red bell pepper, cut into 2" strips
1 large garlic clove, minced
1 tsp. dried basil

1. In a bowl, combine orange juice, stock, vinegar, sugar, orange zest, cornstarch and salt; stir until smooth.
2. In a large nonstick skillet, heat half the oil over high heat. Add chicken; cook, stirring, 3 minutes, or until browned. Transfer to a plate.
3. Add remaining oil to skillet. Add zucchini, red pepper, garlic and basil; cook, stirring, 2 minutes, or until softened. Return chicken to skillet; stir in stock mixture. Cook, stirring occasionally, 2 minutes, or until sauce thickens and vegetables are tender-crisp.

Cal 217 • Fat 8 g

Yield: 4 Servings

Chicken Piri-Piri

Piri-Piri is the name of the hot chiles from Portugal. Unfortunately, they're not always available, but you can add a good pinch of dried chiles to get that fiery flavor. The marinade will keep for a week in a screw-top jar in the fridge and will add flavor to any meat or a pasta sauce, so make a big batch at a time. Also suitable for freezing.

Piri-Piri Marinade

2 small hot red chiles, halved and seeded

1 red bell pepper, halved and seeded

1 to 2 dried chiles (optional)

2 tbsp. red wine vinegar

3 tbsp. olive oil

salt and freshly ground black pepper

4 chicken breasts, skinned

1. **Marinade**: Finely chop chiles and cut red pepper into chunks. Put into a food processor with dried chiles, if using, vinegar, oil, salt and pepper. Whiz until mixed but not smooth.
2. Make 3 to 4 slits into flesh of each chicken breast. Rub ¾ of marinade over each, coating well. Marinate for 30 minutes or overnight, if possible, for a richer flavor.
3. Heat a heavy frying pan, fry chicken for about 6 minutes on each side, turning it once.
4. Drizzle with reserved marinade when serving.
5. Serve with a fresh green salad.

Cal 270 • Fat 15 g

Yield: 4 Servings

Ginger Chicken

Julienned strips of ginger and sliced onions add great flavor and crisp texture to this stir-fried chicken dish.

1 lb. skinless, boneless chicken breasts, cut into ½" cubes

6 garlic cloves, crushed

2 tsp. paprika

1 tsp. turmeric

¾ tsp. salt, or to taste

1 tsp. canola oil

½ tsp. cumin seeds

2 tsp. peeled, julienned ginger

1 medium yellow onion, finely sliced

2 tsp. ground coriander

¼ cup tomato sauce

2 tsp. lemon juice

2 tsp. finely chopped fresh cilantro

1. Place chicken in a bowl. Sprinkle with garlic, paprika, turmeric and salt. Mix to coat chicken. Set aside.
2. Spray a large nonstick skillet with nonstick spray. Add oil and place over medium heat. When oil is hot, add cumin seeds and ginger. Stir-fry 15 to 20 seconds.
3. Stir in onion, reduce heat to medium-low and cover. Cook onion, stirring occasionally, until golden. Add 1 to 2 tbsp. water, as needed, to prevent onion from sticking.
4. Increase heat to medium high; add chicken; stir-fry until cooked on the outside. If necessary, add 1 to 2 spoonfuls water to keep chicken from sticking.
5. Add coriander and tomato sauce. Cook, stirring, for 30 seconds, add 2 tbsp. water and cover. Reduce heat to low; simmer 5 to 7 minutes, until chicken is cooked thoroughly and no pink remains.
6. Uncover and let liquid evaporate, stirring occasionally. Remove from heat, add lemon juice and cilantro; mix well.
7. Transfer to a serving bowl and enjoy warm.

Cal 226 • Fat 6.4 g Yield: 4 Servings

Spicy Hot Chicken Thighs

Pick your hotness level according to your taste buds' tolerance. Choose dried ancho or cascabel peppers for medium-hot, dried cayenne or pasilla peppers for hot, or dried pequín peppers for very hot.

2 fresh hot peppers, such as serrano OR Thai, OR 2 dried hot peppers

6 medium skinless, boneless chicken thighs (about 1¼ lbs. total)

2 tsp. vegetable oil

1 medium onion, chopped (½ cup)

2 garlic cloves, minced

28 oz. can diced tomatoes

1 tbsp. brown sugar

1 tsp. grated ginger

1. Wearing plastic gloves, remove stem and seeds from hot peppers, if using fresh peppers. Cut into small pieces. Set aside.
2. In a large skillet, heat oil and quickly brown chicken thighs on all sides. Remove chicken from skillet. Cook onion and garlic in drippings in skillet until tender. Drain off fat if necessary. Stir in chile peppers, undrained tomatoes, brown sugar and ginger. Bring to a boil.
3. Return chicken thighs to skillet. Return to a boil. Reduce heat. Simmer, covered, for 20 to 30 minutes, or until chicken is tender and no longer pink.

Cal 157 • Fat 7 g

Yield: 6 Servings

Lemon Chicken with Garlic & Potatoes

A great summer roast dinner. For quicker cooking time, joint the chicken, add the potatoes at the start of cooking and roast for 45 minutes.

3½ lb. free-range chicken
good handful of fresh thyme sprigs
large sprig bay leaves
2 lemons
4 tbsp. olive oil
salt and freshly ground black pepper
2 lbs. small new potatoes
1 large head of garlic, unpeeled, halved horizontally

1. Preheat oven to 450°F.
2. Put chicken in a large roasting pan on a bed of thyme sprigs and bay leaves.
3. Zest 1 lemon; set zest aside. Whisk juice of that lemon with oil, salt and pepper; rub over chicken and pour into roasting pan.
4. Place chicken in oven; reduce temperature to 350°F. Cook for 15 minutes. Baste with juices and add potatoes and garlic. Cook for another 30 minutes. Baste chicken and garlic; turn potatoes in juices. Add second lemon, sliced. Cook for another 30 minutes, or until chicken is browned and cooked through.
5. To serve, sprinkle chicken with reserved lemon zest. Carve chicken; serve with roasted garlic, potatoes and pan juices. Accompany with sautéed or roasted zucchini.

Cal 530 • Fat 21 g

Yield: 4 Servings

Tandoori Chicken

In this recipe, the chicken can be cooked on a barbecue. Serve hot or cold with salad, or take on a picnic.

3½ lbs. chicken, jointed into 8 pieces (or 4 boneless breasts, halved or 4 drumsticks and 4 thighs)

1 lemon, juice of

½ tsp. salt

1 onion, peeled and cut into chunks

2 to 3 garlic cloves, peeled and chopped

1" piece fresh ginger, peeled and chopped

1 green chile, seeded and roughly chopped

1 tbsp. ground turmeric

1 tbsp. garam masala

1 tbsp. tomato purée

½ cup natural plain yogurt

1. Cut a few deep slits in chicken; sprinkle all over with lemon juice and salt and leave in a shallow dish for about 30 minutes.
2. Put onion, garlic, ginger and chile into a food processor or blender. Add turmeric, garam masala, tomato purée and yogurt. Whiz to form a paste. Spoon paste over chicken pieces and rub it in. Cover and marinate for at least 2 hours, or overnight if possible.
3. Set oven to 475°F. Put a baking sheet into oven to heat up. Put all chicken pieces on hot baking sheet and bake 15 to 20 minutes.
4. Serve hot or cold with chutney and salad greens, plus a salad of tomato, cucumber and chopped red onion with fresh coriander.

Pictured on page 169.

Cal 310 • Fat 10 g

Yield: 4 Servings

Crispy Oven-Fried Chicken

Colonel Sanders would be proud of our version. Oven-fried means great flavor and much less fat.

1 tbsp. butter
¼ cup 1% milk
1 large egg
1 cup all-purpose flour
1 tsp. garlic powder
1 tsp. paprika
½ tsp. poultry seasoning
1 tsp. salt
¾ tsp. freshly ground pepper
6 skinless chicken breast halves

1. Preheat oven to 350°F. Line a 9 x 13" baking pan with foil and grease foil with 1½ tsp. of shortening.
2. In a medium-sized bowl, blend milk and egg.
3. Combine flour, garlic powder, paprika, poultry seasoning, salt and pepper in a plastic bag or a medium bowl. Shake or toss chicken in flour mixture to coat. Dip chicken into egg mixture, then shake or toss again in flour mixture to coat well.
4. Place chicken in prepared baking pan. Generously spray chicken with nonstick spray. Melt 1½ tsp. shortening and drizzle evenly over chicken.
5. Bake for about 30 minutes. Turn chicken over; bake for 15 to 20 minutes, or until browned on both sides and cooked through. To serve later, let cool, then cover well and refrigerate.

Cal 289 • Fat 12 g

Yield: 6 Servings

Chicken Pot Pie

A quick-method recipe with slow-cooking flavors. This unusual pot-pie recipe has a flaky phyllo crust and a rich-tasting curry filling.

6 baby red potatoes, quartered

1½ cups low-sodium chicken broth

1.8 oz envelope curry sauce mix

1 tbsp. all-purpose flour

1 garlic clove, chopped

½ cup golden raisins

1 cup EACH frozen pearl onions and pea-and-carrot blend, thawed

½ cup dried apricots, cut into strips

10 oz. pkg. fully cooked, honey-roasted boneless chicken breast

6 sheets frozen phyllo dough, thawed

1. Heat oven to 400°F.
2. In 2-quart shallow baking dish, combine potatoes, broth, sauce mix, flour, garlic and raisins; cook in microwave on HIGH, covered, 4 minutes, or until tender, stirring once. Stir in remaining ingredients, except for phyllo.
3. Divide filling among 6 oven-safe individual baking dishes. Spray each phyllo sheet with nonstick spray; roll each diagonally. Wrap phyllo cylinders around inside rim of dishes. Bake 15 minutes, or until golden.

Cal 265 • Fat 4 g

Yield: 6 Servings

Turkey Soft Tacos

These are versatile and a great favorite with all members of the family. They can also be made with ground chicken, beef or pork. You can also substitute pinto beans, lentils or chickpeas for the kidney beans.

1 lb. turkey breast, ground
1 packet taco seasoning mix
1 can kidney beans
6 flour tortillas
¾ cup salsa
6 tbsp. plain nonfat yogurt
½ cup shredded sharp Cheddar cheese
shredded lettuce
chopped fresh tomatoes

1. Combine turkey and taco seasoning; microwave on HIGH, covered, until cooked, about 10 minutes.
2. Meanwhile, rinse beans in a colander under cold running water for 3 minutes. Divide turkey and beans among the tortillas. Top each with 2 tbsp. salsa and 1 tbsp. yogurt, roll up, and sprinkle with cheese. Heat in the microwave.
3. Garnish with shredded lettuce and chopped tomato before serving.

Cal 362 • Fat 9.4 g

Yield: 6 Servings

Tandoori Chicken, page 165
Four Tomato Salad, page 24

Turkey-Mushroom Marsala

Marsala, made from Sicilian grapes, adds a rich smoky flavor to this turkey dish.

4 turkey breast tenderloin steaks (about 1 lb. total)

Mushroom Marsala Marinade

1 cup sliced shiitake mushrooms

⅓ cup dry Marsala OR dry sherry

⅓ cup water

1½ tsp. snipped fresh thyme or ½ tsp. dried thyme, crushed

1 tsp. snipped fresh rosemary or ¼ tsp. dried rosemary, crushed

⅛ tsp. salt

⅛ tsp. cayenne pepper

2 tsp. olive oil

2 tsp. cold water

1 tsp. cornstarch

hot cooked linguine (optional)

chopped fresh rosemary (optional)

1. Rinse turkey; pat dry with paper towels. Place in a plastic bag set in a shallow dish.
2. **Marinade**: Combine all ingredients. Pour over turkey. Close bag. Marinate in refrigerator for 30 minutes or up to 2 hours, turning bag occasionally.
3. Remove turkey from marinade, reserving marinade; pat dry. In a large skillet, heat oil over medium heat. Cook turkey for 8 to 10 minutes, or until tender and no longer pink, turning once. Remove turkey; cover and keep warm. Add marinade to skillet. Bring to a boil. Reduce heat; simmer, covered, for 2 minutes.
4. Stir together water and cornstarch; stir into sauce in skillet. Cook and stir until thickened and bubbly. Cook and stir 2 minutes more.
5. Serve over linguine and sprinkle with rosemary, if desired.

Cal 151 • Fat 5 g

Yield: 4 Servings

Easy Cabbage Rolls

Finally, a recipe that unravels the mystery behind creating ultra-flavorful cabbage rolls without a lot of fuss.

¾ cup chopped onions

1 garlic clove, minced

1½ cups low-sodium, reduced-fat chicken broth

¾ cup long-grain white rice

1 medium head cabbage (about 3 to 4 lbs.)

1½ lbs. lean ground turkey (skinless)

1 egg white

¼ cup chopped fresh parsley

1 tsp. dried marjoram

½ tsp. EACH salt and black pepper

2, 10 oz. cans low-fat condensed tomato soup

1. Spray a medium saucepan with nonstick spray. Add onions and garlic. Cook over medium heat for 2 minutes, stirring often. Add broth and rice; bring to a boil. Reduce heat to medium-low. Cover; cook for 20 to 25 minutes, until rice is tender and liquid absorbed. Stir occasionally.
2. Meanwhile, bring a large pot of water to a boil. Cut cabbage into 8 wedges. Boil cabbage wedges for 5 minutes. Drain. Remove tough inner core. Separate individual leaves and set aside.
3. Combine cooked rice with turkey, egg white, parsley, marjoram, salt and pepper. Mix well (using your hands works best).
4. Spray a 9 x 13" baking pan with nonstick spray. Line bottom with ½ the cabbage leaves. Spread rice/turkey mixture evenly over cabbage. Top with remaining cabbage leaves.
5. Pour soup into a medium bowl. Add 1 can water and mix well. Pour soup evenly over cabbage. Cover and bake for 1 hour at 350°F. Reduce heat to 325°F and cook another 45 minutes. Let cool for 5 minutes before serving.

Cal 258 • Fat 3.3 g

Yield: 8 Servings

Turkey Breast & Chile Salsa

Tangy salsa adds great flavor to baked turkey steaks. Turkey is high in protein and low in fat, plus it is a good source of iron, zinc, phosphorus, potassium and the B vitamins. y

4 turkey breast tenderloin steaks (about 12 oz. total)

½ cup finely crushed reduced-fat salsa-flavored OR reduced-fat cheese-flavored crackers

¼ tsp. ground cumin

¼ tsp. celery seed

1 tbsp. butter, melted

Chile Salsa

14½ oz. can diced tomatoes, drained

4½ oz. can diced green chile peppers, drained

½ cup finely chopped celery

2 to 4 tbsp. snipped fresh cilantro

1 tbsp. red wine vinegar

1 tsp. sugar

⅛ tsp. salt

1. Rinse turkey; pat dry with paper towels. Spray a 2-quart rectangular baking dish with nonstick coating. Set aside.
2. In a shallow dish, combine crushed crackers, cumin and celery seed. Coat turkey with cracker mixture. Place in prepared dish. Drizzle with melted butter. Bake, uncovered, at 375°F about 30 minutes, or until turkey is tender and no longer pink.
3. **Salsa**: In a medium mixing bowl combine drained tomatoes, peppers, celery and cilantro. Stir in vinegar, sugar and salt. Cover and refrigerate until serving time. Serve turkey with the salsa.

Cal 164 • Fat 6 g

Yield: 4 Servings

Stuffed Grilled Turkey Breast

Apricot Walnut Stuffing and a Dijon mustard glaze make this a special-occasion feast.

2 to 2½ lb. bone-in turkey breast half

Apricot Walnut Stuffing

1½ cups soft rye bread crumbs (2 slices)
½ cup snipped dried apricots
¼ cup chopped walnuts, toasted
2 tbsp. apple juice OR water
1 tbsp. virgin olive oil
¼ tsp. dried rosemary, crushed
¼ tsp. garlic salt

¼ tsp. Dijon-style mustard
1 tbsp. water

1. Remove bone from turkey breast. Rinse turkey; pat dry with paper towels. Cut a horizontal slit into thickest part of turkey breast to form a 4 x 5" pocket. Set aside.
2. **Stuffing**: In a medium mixing bowl combine bread crumbs, apricots, walnuts, apple juice, oil, rosemary and garlic salt. Spoon stuffing into pocket. Securely fasten opening with water-soaked wooden toothpicks or tie with heavy cotton string. Stir together mustard and water; set aside.
3. In a covered grill, arrange medium-hot coals around a drip pan. Test for medium heat above drip pan. Place turkey on grill rack over drip pan, but not over coals. Lower grill hood. Grill about 1 hour, or until turkey juices run clear (stuffing should reach 160°F). Brush with mustard mixture during the last 15 minutes of cooking. Cover turkey with foil; let stand for 15 minutes before slicing.

Cal 237 • Fat 11 g | Yield: 8 Servings

201 MORE Fat•Burning RECIPES

BEEF & VEAL

LAMB & PORK

Spicy Beef & Bean Burgers

A burger/burrito – with a tortilla instead of a bun.

1 slightly beaten egg white

½, 15-oz can (¾ cup) pinto beans, rinsed, drained and mashed

¼ cup soft whole-wheat bread crumbs

¼ cup finely chopped celery

1 tbsp. canned diced green chile peppers OR 1 tsp. chopped canned jalapeño peppers

⅛ tsp. garlic powder

1 lb. lean ground beef

8 lettuce leaves

4, 7" flour tortillas, halved

1 cup salsa

1. In a large mixing bowl combine egg white, beans, bread crumbs, celery, peppers and garlic powder. Add ground beef; mix well.
2. Shape meat mixture into eight ½" thick oval patties. Place patties on unheated rack of a broiler pan. Broil 4" from heat for 12 to 14 minutes, or until no longer pink, turning once.
3. To serve, place a lettuce leaf and a burger in the center of each tortilla half. Top burger with 1 tbsp. of salsa. Bring ends of tortilla up and over burger. Top with another tbsp. of salsa.

Cal 185 • Fat 8 g | Yield: 8 Servings

Lasagne

Everybody's favorite comfort food in a lower-fat, flavor-packed recipe.

8 oz. lean ground beef
1 cup chopped onion
2 garlic cloves, minced
16 oz. can tomatoes, undrained and cut up
6 oz. can low-sodium tomato paste
1½ tsp. dried basil, crushed
1½ tsp. dried oregano, crushed
1 tsp. fennel seed, crushed
¼ tsp. salt
9 dried lasagne noodles
12 oz. carton low-fat cottage cheese, drained
1½ cups shredded reduced-fat mozzarella cheese (6 oz.)
¼ cup grated Parmesan cheese (1 oz.)
1 egg
2 tbsp. snipped fresh parsley
pepper to taste

1. In a saucepan, cook beef, onion and garlic until meat is browned. Drain off fat. Stir in tomatoes, tomato paste, basil, oregano, fennel seed and salt. Bring to a boil; reduce heat. Simmer, covered, for 15 minutes, stirring occasionally.
2. Meanwhile, cook lasagne noodles according to package directions. Drain; rinse with cold water. Drain well.
3. For filling, combine cottage cheese, 1 cup mozzarella, Parmesan, egg, parsley and pepper.
4. Layer ⅓ of cooked noodles in a 2-quart rectangular baking dish, trimming ends to fit. Spread with ½ of filling. Top with ⅓ of sauce. Repeat layers. Top with remaining noodles and sauce. Sprinkle with remaining mozzarella.
5. Bake, uncovered, at 375°F for 30 to 35 minutes, or until heated through. Let stand 10 minutes before serving.

Cal 281 • Fat 8 g

Yield: 8 Servings

Moussaka

Be sure to use a low-fat or partly skimmed-milk cheese to reduce fat in this light version of a typical Greek dish.

1 eggplant, about 1 to 1½ lbs., sliced

salt

olive oil

2 tsp. dried basil, oregano, rosemary OR thyme (optional)

minced garlic (optional)

1. **Baked Eggplant**: Often we pass up eggplant because it soaks up too much fat while cooking. To make baked eggplant, salt cut surfaces and let slices drain in a colander for 30 minutes to reduce amount of oil absorbed in cooking. Rinse off salt under cold water; drain on paper towels and pat dry.
2. Lightly brush eggplant slices with oil, sprinkle with basil, oregano, rosemary or thyme for extra flavor. Minced garlic can be sprinkled over top of slices before baking. Bake in a single layer at 425°F until lightly browned and tender. Depending on their size and ripeness, slices will take 20 to 35 minutes to cook. Turn occasionally for even browning.

Cal 328 • Fat 15.8 g

Yield: 6 Servings

Moussaka

Continued

1 tbsp. olive oil

1 medium onion, chopped

1 lb. lean ground beef OR lamb

14 oz. can tomato sauce

½ cup dry red wine OR beef stock

½ tsp. dried thyme

¼ tsp. cinnamon

1 cup shredded Monterey Jack OR mozzarella cheese

2 tbsp. chopped fresh parsley

3. In a large skillet, heat oil; add onion and cook over medium heat until onion is softened but not browned. Stir in beef; cook until crumbly and browned.
4. Stir in tomato sauce, wine, thyme and cinnamon; simmer, uncovered, for 10 minutes, stirring occasionally.
5. In a 7 x 11" baking dish, arrange half of baked eggplant slices. Top with meat mixture, then remaining eggplant. Sprinkle with cheese and parsley. Bake at 375°F for about 20 minutes, or until bubbly and golden.

Stir-Fried Beef with Peppers & Snow Peas

French cooks call snow peas mange-tout *(eat it all). Choose thin, crisp almost translucent pea pods that are bright green with very small, tender peas.*

½ lb. flank steak, trimmed of all visible fat

3 tsp. reduced-sodium soy sauce

1 tbsp. peanut oil

1 scallion, the white and part of the green, minced

1 to 2 tbsp. finely slivered fresh ginger

1 garlic clove, minced

½ sweet red pepper, cut into ½" strips

15 snow peas (about 2 ozs.), tops and strings removed

1 tbsp. oyster sauce (found in Oriental stores)

1. Holding a sharp knife at a 45°F angle, slice steak into thin strips. In a bowl, toss with 1 tsp. of soy sauce. Let stand for 20 minutes.
2. Heat a large, heavy skillet or wok over high heat for 30 seconds. Add oil and swirl to coat surface of pan evenly. Continue heating until oil just starts to smoke.
3. Add scallions, ginger and garlic and stir-fry until fragrant, about 20 seconds. Add beef and stir-fry until lightly browned, about 1 minute. Add pepper strips and snow peas; stir-fry until peppers wilt, about 20 seconds. Stir in remaining 2 tsp. soy sauce and oyster sauce. Cook and stir just until meat is cooked through, about 1 minute.
4. Serve immediately with rice.

Cal 273 • Fat 15 g Yield: 2 Servings

London Broil

Flank steak is one exception to the rule that meat should be brought to room temperature before cooking. Serve this with ratatouille, page 85, or sliced tomatoes, purple onions and cucumbers, almost any vegetable would make a good accompaniment.

Garlic Ginger Marinade

½ cup reduced-sodium soy sauce

¼ cup dry red wine

freshly ground black pepper

fresh ginger, about the size of your first thumb joint, grated or finely chopped

4 garlic cloves, finely chopped

2½ lbs. flank steak, "Choice" grade, trimmed of all fat, or first-cut top round, very well-trimmed of fat

1. **Marinade:** In a glass baking dish, combine soy sauce, wine, pepper, grated ginger and garlic. Marinate flank steak in marinade for several hours, turning occasionally. Keep refrigerated until cooking time.
2. To cook, preheat broiler. Remove steak from marinade and broil quickly, about 5 to 6 minutes per side.
3. Remove steak to a cutting board. Holding a well-sharpened carving knife at an angle, and almost flat along the top of the meat, slice thinly on the diagonal through to the bottom. Meat should be rare in the center.

Cal 175 • Fat 8 g

Yield: 10 Servings

Best Bistro-Style Steak

Beef is back and that includes the mighty steak, but in well-trimmed portions. Dressed up with wine, garlic and herbs, this steak recipe becomes a special dish when you're entertaining friends.

4, 6 oz. boneless strip-loin steaks

½ tsp. coarsely ground black pepper

2 tsp. olive oil

2 tsp. butter

salt

¼ cup finely chopped shallots

1 large clove garlic, finely chopped

pinch EACH of thyme, rosemary and basil

⅓ cup red wine OR additional stock

½ cup beef stock

1 tbsp. Dijon mustard

2 tbsp. chopped parsley

1. Remove steaks from refrigerator 30 minutes before cooking. Season with pepper.
2. Heat a large heavy skillet over medium heat until hot; add oil and butter. Increase heat to high; brown steaks 1 minute per side. Reduce heat to medium; cook steaks to desired degree of doneness. Transfer to a heated serving platter. Season to taste with salt; keep warm.
3. Add shallots, garlic and herbs to skillet; cook, stirring, for 1 minute. Add red wine; cook, scraping up any brown bits from bottom of pan, until liquid has almost evaporated.
4. Add stock, mustard and parsley; season to taste with salt and pepper. Cook, stirring, until slightly reduced. Spoon sauce over steaks. Serve immediately.

Cal 329 • Fat 15 g

Yield: 4 Servings

Veal with Pineapple-Lime-Pecan Sauce

Use chicken, pork or turkey scallopini to replace veal. Use frozen juice concentrate and freeze remaining juice. Orange juice can also be used. If limes are unavailable, use lemons.

1 lb. veal scallopini

2 tsp. oil

3 tbsp. flour

Pineapple-Lime-Pecan Sauce

¼ cup chopped green onions (about 2 medium)

2 tbsp. chopped pecans

¼ cup pineapple juice concentrate

¼ cup water

1 tbsp. honey

1 tbsp. fresh lime juice

1 tsp. grated lime zest

1. Between sheets of waxed paper, pound veal to ¼" (6 mm) thickness.
2. In a large nonstick skillet sprayed with nonstick spray, heat oil over medium-high heat. Dredge veal in flour and cook for 2 minutes per side, or until just done at the center. Place on a serving dish and cover.
3. **Sauce**: Add green onions and pecans to skillet. Cook 2 minutes. Add pineapple juice concentrate, water, honey, lime juice and lime zest. Bring to a boil for 1 minute, or until slightly syrupy and thickened. Serve sauce over veal.

Cal 217 • Fat 6 g

Yield: 4 Servings

Veal Chops & Sage Dressing

Treat family and friends to a tempting meal: juicy veal chops topped with a sage-seasoned apple dressing, then simmered in white wine and chicken broth. Delicious!!!

1 large onion, chopped

1½ cups low-sodium chicken broth

4 cups cubed whole-wheat bread (½" cubes; you'll need 4 slices)

2 stalks celery, thinly sliced

1 large tart green-skinned apple such as Granny Smith OR Newtown Pippin (about 8 oz.) cored and chopped

1 cup raisins

1 tsp. dried sage

4 lean veal loin chops (about 1½ lbs. total), trimmed of fat

½ cup dry white wine

1. Place onion and ½ cup broth in a wide nonstick skillet. Cook over high heat, stirring often, until onion is soft and liquid has evaporated, about 5 minutes.
2. Scrape onion into a large bowl; add ½ cup broth, bread, celery, apple, raisins and sage. Mix well.
3. Add veal chops to skillet and cook over medium-high heat, turning once, until well browned on both sides, about 5 minutes.
4. Mound dressing evenly over chops. Pour wine and remaining ½ cup broth around chops; bring to a boil. Reduce heat to low, cover and simmer until veal is very tender when pierced, about 35 minutes.

Cal 349 • Fat 5 g

Yield: 4 Servings

Lamb Curry

This mildly spiced curry dish is a wonderful choice to serve family and guests.

12 oz. trimmed lamb from leg, cut into ½" pieces

Yogurt Marinade

1 cup plain nonfat yogurt

1 medium yellow onion, very finely chopped

½ tsp. grated ginger

4 garlic cloves, crushed

2 tsp. paprika

2 medium potatoes, cut into 1" cubes

1 medium tomato, very finely chopped

½ tsp. salt, or to taste

¼ tsp. homemade garam masala OR commercial variety

1 tbsp. finely chopped fresh cilantro

1. Place lamb in a medium-sized mixing bowl.
2. Combine marinade ingredients and add to lamb; stir to coat. Cover and refrigerate 2 to 3 hours.
3. Place potatoes in a medium-sized bowl. Add cold water to cover potatoes; set aside.
3. Spray a large nonstick wok or skillet with nonstick spray; place over medium-high heat. When hot, add lamb and marinade, stir well. When it begins to bubble, reduce heat to medium-low and cover. Cook, stirring often, about 45 minutes.
4. Drain potatoes, reserving ¾ cup of soaking water. Add potatoes, soaking water and tomato to lamb. Cover and simmer 15 to 20 minutes, until lamb is completely cooked, potatoes are tender and curry is slightly thickened.
5. Remove from heat; stir in salt and garam masala.
6. Transfer to a serving dish; sprinkle with cilantro and serve hot.

Cal 203 • Fat 5.1 g

Yield: 5 Servings

Pork Lo Mein (Chinese Noodles with Pork)

4 to 5 dried black Chinese mushrooms (optional)

½ lb. lean pork loin OR roast pork

1 head napa (Chinese) cabbage

2 to 3 whole scallions

2 tbsp. peanut OR olive oil

½ tsp. salt

1 lb. spaghetti OR Chinese noodles, parboiled, drained and rinsed to stop cooking

2 tbsp. sodium-reduced soy sauce, preferably Chinese OR Tamari

1. Soak mushrooms in warm water 30 to 60 minutes. Drain, rinse and squeeze dry. Remove stems and reserve for soup.
2. Slice pork thinly and shred into matchstick-sized strips. Cut cabbage crosswise into 1" pieces. Cut scallions into 1" sections. Slice mushrooms thinly.
3. Heat oil until very hot in a wok or large heavy skillet. Add salt, then scallions and stir-fry for about 45 seconds. Add pork strips and stir-fry until they lose their pinkness, 2 to 3 minutes. If using roast pork, stir-fry for 45 seconds.
4. Add cabbage and mushrooms and stir-fry with a scoop-and-toss motion for 2 minutes more. Add parboiled noodles and soy sauce and toss gently. Cover wok or skillet and cook 5 minutes over medium heat, or until noodles are warmed through.

Cal 340 • Fat 7 g | Yield: 6 to 8 Servings

Saucy Asian Pork Stir-Fry

Roasted peanuts, along with ginger and garlic, add crunch and freshness to the richly flavored sauce in this quick and easy main dish. No ordering out!

½ cup long-grain rice

10 oz. can condensed French onion soup

1 tbsp. peanut oil

2 garlic cloves, minced

1 tsp. grated fresh ginger

⅛ tsp. crushed red pepper flakes

16 oz. pkg. frozen stir-fry vegetables, such as snap peas, onions, mushrooms and carrots

1 lb. pork tenderloin, cut into 1" cubes

1 tbsp. soy sauce

¼ cup unsalted cocktail peanuts

1. Cook rice according to package directions, without butter and salt, using 1 cup water and ⅓ cup undiluted soup.
2. Meanwhile, in a large skillet heat oil over medium-high heat. Add garlic, ginger and pepper flakes; cook 1 minute.
3. Stir in vegetables; cook, stirring, until heated through, 3-4 minutes. Remove from skillet; reserve.
4. Add pork to skillet; cook, stirring, until lightly browned, about 1 minute. Stir in soy sauce; cook until meat is no longer pink in center, 4 to 5 minutes.
5. Return vegetables to skillet. Stir in remaining soup; heat through, 2 to 3 minutes. Transfer rice to a serving platter. Top with pork. Sprinkle with peanuts.

Cal 397 • Fat 12 g

Yield: 4 Servings

Grilled Pork Tenderloin

Extremely easy and utterly delicious! The medallions go well with rice or sweet potatoes.

2 lbs. lean pork tenderloin, all visible fat removed

¼ cup white vinegar

½ cup reduced-sodium soy sauce

2 tbsp. minced garlic

freshly ground black pepper to taste

1 tsp. dried hot red pepper flakes

1. Cut pork into ½" thick medallions.
2. In a rectangular glass baking dish, mix together vinegar, soy sauce, garlic and pepper. Add pork and marinate 4 to 5 hours in the refrigerator, turning occasionally.
3. Preheat broiler. Broil medallions 7 minutes on each side about 4" from flame. (These are also delicious on a charcoal grill; cook over a medium fire 5 minutes on each side, then 10 minutes covered).
4. While pork is cooking, bring marinade to a boil in a small saucepan. Add hot pepper flakes and reduce by one quarter. Strain and serve as a dipping sauce with pork.

Cal 185 • Fat 4 g Yield: 6 Servings

Mustard-Orange Pork Tenderloin

Sweet and tangy, this glaze is superb with the pork and with the mushrooms.

12 oz. pork tenderloin

Apricot Dijon Glaze

½ cup apricot preserves OR orange marmalade
3 tbsp. Dijon-style mustard

2 cups sliced fresh mushrooms
½ cup sliced green onions
2 tbsp. orange juice

1. Trim any fat from tenderloin. Place in a shallow roasting pan. Insert a meat thermometer. Roast, uncovered, at 425°F for 10 minutes.
2. **Glaze**: In a small mixing bowl, stir together preserves and mustard.
3. Spoon half of glaze over tenderloin; set remaining glaze aside. Roast for 15 to 25 minutes more, or until thermometer registers 160°F. Cover meat with foil and let stand for 5 minutes before carving.
4. Spray a medium saucepan with nonstick coating. Add mushrooms and onions. Cook and stir for 2 to 3 minutes, or until mushrooms are tender. Stir in remaining mustard glaze and orange juice. Cook and stir until heated through.
5. To serve, thinly slice tenderloin. Spoon mushrooms over tenderloin.

Cal 240 • Fat 4 g

Yield: 4 Servings

Mustard Pork with Prunes

Mustard seeds give a crunchy coating to the pork, without adding a strong mustard flavor, while prunes add rich sweetness.

1 cup pitted prunes
½ cup chopped sweet red pepper
⅓ cup chopped green onions
¼ cup chopped fresh parsley
2 pork tenderloins (about ¾ lb.)
Dijon mustard
¼ cup mustard seeds
1 tsp. coarse cracked black pepper

1. In a saucepan, bring prunes and ½ cup water to a boil; reduce heat and simmer 5 minutes. Drain off excess liquid. Add red pepper, onions and parsley; mix well.
2. Make a horizontal cut in the center, along the side of each tenderloin; open and spread flat, like a book.
3. Spread 1 tenderloin with prune mixture. Top with second tenderloin, positioning it with thickest end on top of thinnest end of first. Tie together in 3 or 4 places. Spread a thin layer of mustard over top of tenderloin.
4. Spread mustard seeds on waxed paper; sprinkle pepper over top. Place stuffed loin, mustard-coated side down, on seed mixture. Spread mustard on uncoated side. Turn roll over to coat second side with seed mixture. Place in a greased baking pan.
5. Roast at 425°F for 30 minutes; turn and roast for 15 minutes longer, or until meat thermometer inserted in meat (not stuffing) registers 175°F.

Cal 242 • Fat 6.4 g — Yield: 6 Servings

201 MORE Fat•Burning RECIPES

DESSERTS & SWEETS

Baked Ginger Pears

Baked with a little sugar and a generous helping of crystallized ginger, these juicy whole pears are delightful for a cool-weather dessert. You might serve this spicy fruit with spoonfuls of vanilla frozen yogurt.

6 medium firm-ripe Bosc OR Bartlett pears (about 2½ lbs. total)

¾ cup water

1 tbsp. lemon juice

2 tbsp. sugar

⅓ cup minced crystallized ginger

vanilla low-fat frozen yogurt (optional)

1. If necessary, trim bottoms of pears so they will stand upright. Fit pears snugly into a shallow 1½ to 2 quart baking dish (such as an 8"square baking pan).
2. In a small bowl, mix water and lemon juice; pour over pears. Sprinkle with sugar.
3. Bake, uncovered, at 450°F for 30 minutes; reduce oven temperature to 400°F. Baste pears with pan juices, sprinkle with ginger and continue to bake, basting occasionally, until pears are richly browned and tender when pierced, 30 to 45 minutes.
4. Serve warm or cool. Top with frozen yogurt, if desired.

Cal 167 • Fat 0.7 g

Yield: 6 Servings

Stuffed Baked Apple

Next time you are baking a roast or casserole, make one or more of these and put them in the oven for dessert.

1 small apple, cored
1 tbsp. raisins
1 tsp. lemon juice
½ tsp. shredded coconut
½ tsp. honey
dash ground cinnamon
1 tsp. water

1. Core apple and pare ⅓ of the way down.
2. In a small bowl, combine remaining ingredients, except water. Stuff into cored apple. Place water in bottom of an ovenproof custard cup; add filled apple, cover with foil.
3. Bake at 350°F for 35 to 45 minutes.

Cal 114 • Fat 1 g — Yield: 1 Serving

Stewed Dried Apricots

Delicious with low-fat frozen yogurt or plain low-fat yogurt.

8 medium dried apricot halves
1 cup water
1 tbsp. lemon juice
1 cinnamon stick

1. Place apricots in a small saucepan. Add remaining ingredients; simmer for 20 minutes. Remove cinnamon stick.

Cal 39 • Fat 0.1 g — Yield: 2 Servings

Pavlova

Pavlova is an elegant light dessert made with a meringue base covered with fresh fruit and whipped topping. Regular whipping cream has a whopping 88 g of fat per cup! That's why using a light whipped topping or frozen yogurt makes a lot of sense.

4 egg whites

1 cup sugar

½ tsp. vanilla

1 tbsp. vinegar

2½ cups light whipped topping OR frozen yogurt

¼ cup toasted sliced almonds

fresh fruit such as sliced strawberries, papaya, kiwi OR blueberries

1. In a glass bowl, whip egg whites until soft peaks form. Beat in sugar, vanilla and vinegar. Whip until stiff peaks form.
2. Line a baking sheet with parchment or brown paper. Spread meringue mixture onto paper in a flat round shape.
3. Bake at 275°F for 1 hour. Turn oven off and leave meringue in oven until oven is cool (several hours).
4. Just before serving, top with whipped topping, fresh fruit and toasted almonds.

Cal 229 • Fat 8 g

Yield: 8 Servings

Strawberry Cheesecake

To test for a perfectly baked, creamy cheesecake, gently shake the pan after the minimum baking time. The center should appear nearly set. If it still jiggles, bake it 5 minutes longer and test again.

½ cup graham cracker crumbs
4 tsp. melted butter
1 cup fat-free cottage cheese
¼ cup skim milk
2, 8 oz. pkgs. fat-free cream cheese, cut up
¾ cup sugar
2 tbsp. all-purpose flour
1¼ tsp. vanilla
½ tsp. finely shredded lemon zest
3 eggs OR ¾ cup refrigerated or frozen egg product, thawed
¼ cup fat-free or light dairy sour cream
1 tsp. sugar
2 tsp. skim milk
1 cup sliced fresh strawberries

1. In a small bowl, combine crumbs and melted butter. Press into an 8" springform pan. Set aside.
2. In a large food processor, place undrained cottage cheese and ¼ cup milk; cover; process until smooth. Add cream cheese, ¾ cup sugar, flour, 1 tsp. vanilla and lemon zest; cover and process until smooth. Add eggs and process just until combined. Do not over process. Pour into pan. Place on a baking sheet.
3. Bake at 375°F for 35 to 40 minutes; until set. Cool 15 minutes. Using a narrow metal spatula, loosen cheesecake from pan ring. Cool 30 minutes more, remove pan ring. Cool completely. Cover; refrigerate at least 4 hours.
4. In a bowl combine sour cream, 1 tsp. sugar, milk and vanilla. To serve, arrange berries on cheesecake; drizzle with sour cream mixture.

Pictured on page 203.

Cal 163• Fat 3 g

Yield: 12 Servings

Pumpkin Pie

Enjoy this lighter version of a traditional favorite. Besides being delicious, pumpkin is loaded with beta-carotene, an important antioxidant. A gingersnap crumb crust is a delicious variation for Pumpkin Pie.

15 oz. can pumpkin purée

¾ cup fat-free half-and-half cream

½ cup sugar

2 eggs, slightly beaten

¾ tsp. ground cinnamon

¼ tsp. ground cloves

¼ tsp. ground ginger

⅛ tsp. ground nutmeg

8" prepared pie crust

1. Preheat oven to 425°F.
2. In a medium bowl, with an electric mixer on medium speed, combine all ingredients, except pie crust, and beat until well blended.
3. Pour filling into prepared crust and bake for 15 minutes. Reduce temperature to 350°F and bake until center is firm, about 45 minutes.
4. Serve chilled.

Cal 237 • Fat 10 g

Yield: 8 Servings

Bing Cherry Flan

In central France, this custardy fruit dessert is known as clafoutis. It can be made with a variety of fresh fruits – plums, pears, peaches – but plump, glossy dark sweet cherries are the traditional first choice.

2 cups dark sweet cherries, stemmed and pitted
2 tbsp. kirsch OR brandy
2 tbsp. all-purpose flour
⅓ cup sugar
⅛ tsp ground nutmeg
1 large egg
2 large egg whites
1½ cups evaporated skim milk
1 tsp. vanilla
2 tbsp. powdered sugar

1. Spray a 10" quiche dish or other shallow 1½-quart baking dish with nonstick spray. Spread cherries in dish; drizzle with kirsch and set aside.
2. In a medium-sized bowl, combine flour, sugar and nutmeg. Beat in egg, then egg whites; gradually stir in milk and vanilla. Pour egg mixture over cherries.
3. Bake at 350°F until custard is puffed and golden brown, and a knife inserted in center comes out clean, about 45 minutes.
4. Let cool slightly, then sift powdered sugar over top. Cut into wedges and serve warm.

Cal 174 • Fat 2 g

Yield: 6 Servings

Apple Cake

Instead of making apple pie, which is usually high in fat, make scrumptious apple cake to use up all those apples in the fall. The best baking and cooking apples include: Fuji, Granny Smith, McIntosh, Newton Pippin, Rome Beauty and Winesap. I pound of apples = 2 large, 3 medium or 4 to 5 small; I pound of apples = 3 cups of peeled, sliced apples.

1¼ cups flour
½ cup sugar
1 tsp. cinnamon
1 tsp. baking soda
¼ cup chopped walnuts
½ tsp. salt (optional)
2 cups peeled, grated apples
1 egg white, beaten
¼ cup vegetable oil

1. In a mixing bowl, combine flour, sugar, cinnamon, baking soda, walnuts and salt. Mix well. Add apples, egg white and oil. Stir until combined. Batter will be very thick.
2. Spray a 8 x 10" baking pan or 10" round springform pan with nonstick spray and pour batter into pan.
3. Bake at 350°F for 30 to 35 minutes, or until done.

Cal 141 • Fat 5 g

Yield: 12 Servings

Maple-Pineapple Upside-Down Cake

This moist cake is flavored with maple syrup and vanilla. Pineapple is traditionally the most popular flavor for upside-down cakes.

1 cup brown sugar
¼ cup maple syrup
½ cup skim milk
10 water-packed canned pineapple slices, drained, ½ cup liquid reserved
1 cup white sugar
2 egg whites
2 tsp. vanilla extract
1½ cups all-purpose flour
½ tsp. baking powder

1. Preheat oven to 325°F.
2. Mix brown sugar, maple syrup and ¼ cup milk; spread evenly in a 9 x 13" nonstick baking dish.
3. Cut pineapple slices in half and arrange in a single layer on top of brown sugar mixture.
4. Combine reserved pineapple liquid, sugar, egg whites, vanilla and remaining milk; mix thoroughly. Combine flour and baking powder and stir into egg white mixture until dry ingredients are completely incorporated.
5. Pour batter over pineapple slices in baking dish and bake until done, about 35 minutes.
6. Allow to cool for 10 minutes. Turn out onto a plate and serve.

Cal 247 • Fat 0 g

Yield: 12 Servings

Sour Cream Coffee Cake

This is one of Rene's favorite cakes. It's basic, simple and filled with whole-grain goodness. For variety, try adding chopped fruit to the batter before baking it.

Cake

1½ cups whole-wheat pastry flour

1 cup sugar

2 tsp. baking powder

1 tsp. baking soda

1 cup nonfat sour cream

2 eggs, lightly beaten

½ tsp. vanilla

¼ tsp. orange extract

Brown Sugar Pecan Topping

2 tbsp. whole-wheat pastry flour

5 tbsp. brown sugar

2 tbsp. chopped pecans

1 tbsp. unsalted butter

1. Preheat oven to 350°F. Lightly spray an 8" square baking pan with nonstick spray.
2. **Cake**: In a large bowl, combine flour, sugar, baking powder and baking soda. In a medium bowl, whisk together sour cream, eggs, vanilla and orange extract. Pour into flour mixture and stir until combined. Pour batter into pan and set aside.
3. **Topping**: In a blender or food processor, combine flour, brown sugar, pecans and butter. Blend until mixture forms fine crumbs. Sprinkle over batter.
4. Bake for 35 minutes, or until center looks set and a toothpick inserted into center comes out moist but not wet. Cool on a rack before slicing.

Cal 136 • Fat 2.1 g

Yield: 16 Servings

Sour Cream Fudge Cake

Try replacing the butter, margarine or other solid shortening in cakes, muffins, breads, biscuits, quick breads, crisp cookies, tender pie crusts and other treats with half as much vegetable oil. *For instance, if a recipe calls for ½ cup of butter, use ¼ cup of oil instead. Bake as usual, checking for doneness a few minutes before the end of the usual baking time. This technique makes it possible to produce moist and tender baked products with about half the original fat.*

1½ cups unbleached flour
¾ cup oat flour
1½ cups sugar
¾ cup cocoa powder
2 tsp. baking soda
¼ tsp. salt
1 cup coffee, cooled to temperature
1 cup unsweetened applesauce
½ cup fat-free egg substitute OR 2 egg whites, lightly beaten
2 tsp. vanilla extract

Chocolate Glaze

1¼ cups powdered sugar
¼ cup nonfat sour cream
2 tbsp. cocoa powder
1 tsp. vanilla extract

1. Place flours, sugar, cocoa, baking soda and salt in a large bowl; mix well.
2. Place coffee, applesauce, sour cream, egg substitute and vanilla in a medium-sized bowl; mix well with a whisk. Add coffee mixture to flour mixture; whisk well.
3. Coat a 9 x 13" pan with nonstick spray; pour batter into pan. Bake at 325°F for 35 minutes, or until top springs back when touched and a toothpick inserted in center of cake comes out clean. Don't overbake. Remove cake from oven; set aside.
4. **Glaze**: In a small bowl, combine all ingredients until smooth. Add more sour cream if needed to make a thick frosting. Spread glaze over hot cake.
5. Allow cake to cool to room temperature before cutting in squares and serving.

Cal 194 • Fat 1 g

Yield: 16 Servings

Fudge Marble Cake

⅔ cup oat bran

1 cup + 2 tbsp. nonfat or low-fat buttermilk

2⅓ cups unbleached flour

1 tsp. baking soda

¼ lb. (1 stick) light butter OR reduced-fat margarine at room temperature

1½ cups sugar

¼ cup + 2 tbsp. fat-free egg substitute

2½ tsp. vanilla extract

Fudge Marble

¼ cup Dutch processed cocoa powder

¼ cup chocolate syrup

Chocolate Glaze

½ cup powdered sugar

1 tbsp. Dutch processed cocoa powder

1 tbsp. skim milk

½ tsp. vanilla extract

1. In a small bowl, whisk oat bran and buttermilk together. Set aside for at least 10 minutes.
2. Combine flour and baking soda in a medium bowl. Set aside.
3. Place butter in a large bowl; beat with an electric mixer until smooth. Beat in sugar, ½ cup at a time. Beat in egg substitute and vanilla.
4. Add flour and oat bran mixtures to butter mixture; stir well. Set aside.
5. **Fudge Marble**: Place 1 cup of cake batter in a small bowl. Stir in cocoa and chocolate syrup.
6. Spray a 12-cup bundt pan with nonstick spray; fill ¾ with white batter. Top with all chocolate batter and finish off with remaining white batter.
7. Bake at 350°F for 43 minutes, or until a toothpick inserted in center comes out clean. Be careful not to overbake. Cool in pan for 40 minutes. Invert onto a serving platter; cool to room temperature.
8. **Glaze**: Place all ingredients in a small bowl; mix well. Drizzle glaze over cooled cake. Allow to sit for 15 minutes before slicing and serving.

Cal 182 • Fat 3 g

Yield: 18 Servings

Strawberry Cheesecake, page 195

Fresh Start Chocolate Cake

Spectacular, super moist and chocolaty, you won't believe this cake is low in fat. Kids will love it!

1 cup all-purpose flour
⅓ cup unsweetened cocoa powder
1½ tsp. baking powder
1 tsp. baking soda
¾ tsp. cinnamon
¼ tsp. salt
1¼ cups packed brown sugar
1 egg
2 egg whites
3 tbsp. canola OR vegetable oil
1 tsp. vanilla
¼ tsp. almond extract
1 cup low-fat sour cream
½ cup mini chocolate chips

1. Preheat oven to 350°F.
2. In a small bowl, mix together flour, cocoa, baking powder, baking soda, cinnamon and salt. Set aside.
3. In a medium bowl, with an electric mixer on medium speed, blend together brown sugar, egg, egg whites and oil. Add vanilla, almond extract and sour cream. Beat on low speed until well-blended.
4. Gradually add flour mixture to sour cream mixture, beating on medium speed. Fold in chocolate chips.
5. Spray an 8" square pan with nonstick spray. Spread batter evenly in pan. Bake for 40 to 45 minutes, until a wooden pick inserted in center comes out clean. Check cake after 40 minutes; don't overbake.
6. Remove from oven and cool in pan 15 minutes. Cut into 12 squares. For maximum moistness, store at room temperature in an airtight container.

Cal 218 • Fat 6.6 g

Yield: 12 Servings

Fudge Brownies

For delectable low-fat chocolate desserts, cocoa is your best friend. One ounce of chocolate contains as much as 16 grams of fat per ounce, a comparable amount of cocoa powder has only 3 grams. ***To substitute cocoa powder for chocolate in baking, use 3 tbsp. unsweetened cocoa powder plus 1 tbsp. of water in place of each 1 oz. square of unsweetened chocolate. If the recipe calls for semisweet chocolate, also add 1 tbsp. sugar for each ounce of chocolate.***

1 cup all-purpose flour

1 cup packed brown sugar

¾ cup white sugar

½ cup unsweetened cocoa powder

½ tsp. baking powder

½ cup refrigerated or frozen egg product, thawed

⅓ cup unsweetened applesauce

¼ cup butter OR margarine, melted

1 tsp. vanilla

¼ cup chopped walnuts

1 tbsp. powdered sugar OR chocolate-flavored syrup (optional)

1. Spray a 3-quart rectangular baking pan with nonstick coating. Set aside.
2. In a large mixing bowl, stir together flour, brown sugar, white sugar, cocoa and baking powder. Stir in egg product, applesauce, butter and vanilla just until combined. Spread evenly in pan. Sprinkle with walnuts.
3. Bake at 350°F about 20 minutes, or until center appears set. Cool on a wire rack.
4. If desired sprinkle with powdered sugar or drizzle with chocolate-flavored syrup. To serve, cut into bars.

Cal 10 • Fat 3 g

Yield: 24 Servings

Chocolate Delights

Surprise! Chocolate is one of the most healthy antioxidants around. Our moist, dense Chocolate Delights pack a powerful chocolate punch, without too much fat, thanks to the clever mixing of cocoa powder (chocolate with much of the fat removed); yes there is a God!

4 squares semisweet chocolate (4 oz.)

⅓ cup cocoa powder

¾ cup sugar

½ cup evaporated fat-free milk

2 large egg yolks

½ tsp. vanilla extract (optional)

3 large egg whites, at room temperature

¼ cup all-purpose flour

½ tsp. baking powder

12 strawberries

1. Preheat oven to 350°F. Line a 12-cup muffin/cupcake pan with foil liners.
2. Place chocolate in a large microwaveable bowl. Microwave on high for 2 minutes to melt; stir until smooth. Set aside.
3. In a small saucepan, whisk together cocoa and ½ cup sugar. Mix in milk. Cook for 2 minutes over medium heat, whisking constantly until smooth. Stir cocoa mixture into melted chocolate. Stir in egg yolks and vanilla.
4. In a large bowl, on medium speed, beat egg whites until foamy. Gradually add ¼ cup sugar. Increase speed to high; beat just until stiff.
5. Fold egg whites into chocolate mixture ⅓ at a time. Fold in flour and baking powder. Divide batter evenly among muffin cups.
6. Bake 20 to 22 minutes, or until a toothpick inserted into the center comes out clean. Cool.
7. Top each cake with a strawberry.

Cal 133 • Fat 4 g

Yield: 12 Servings

Mom's Chewy Chocolate Cookies

These are a favorite at my house and I bet they will be at yours too.

5 tbsp. butter, softened
7 tbsp. fat-free cream cheese
2 cups sugar
1 egg
2 egg whites
1 tbsp. vanilla extract
2 cups all-purpose flour
¾ cup cocoa powder
1 tsp. baking soda
½ tsp. salt
1⅓ cups (8 oz.) semisweet chocolate chips
1 cup chopped walnuts (optional)

1. Preheat oven to 350°F. Coat 2 cookie sheets with nonstick spray.
2. In a large bowl, cream butter and cream cheese together. Add sugar and beat until creamy. Add egg, egg whites and vanilla; beat until smooth.
3. Combine flour, cocoa, baking soda and salt in a medium bowl. Add to butter mixture and beat until blended. Stir in chocolate chips and walnuts, if desired. Drop by teaspoonfuls onto prepared cookie sheets.
3. Bake, 1 cookie sheet at a time, in top third of oven, for about 8 minutes; do not overbake. Remove from cookie sheet; let cool on a wire rack.

Note: To make larger cookies, use a cookie scoop to form cookies. Bake for about 10 minutes. (This will yield about 2½ dozen cookies.)

Cal 122 • Fat 2.2 g

Yield: About 4 dozen

Molasses Cookies

Cinnamon, ginger and cloves make these spicy molasses cookies special. Dark molasses NOT blackstrap molasses, is best for baking. Unsulphered molasses is lighter and has a cleaner, nicer flavor. Molasses is a by-product from the refining of sugar cane and sugar beets.

¼ cup unsalted butter OR coconut oil (organic)

¾ cup honey

½ cup molasses

1 egg OR ¼ cup fat-free egg substitute

2½ cups whole-wheat pastry flour

1½ tsp. ground cinnamon

1 tsp. ground ginger

1 tsp. baking soda

¼ tsp. ground cloves

½ cup nonfat buttermilk

1. Preheat oven to 350°F. Lightly coat 2 baking sheets with nonstick spray.
2. In a large bowl, using an electric mixer, cream butter until smooth. Beat in honey, molasses and egg. Set aside.
3. In another large bowl, combine flour, cinnamon, ginger, baking soda and cloves.
4. Beat flour mixture and buttermilk into egg mixture. Stir until well mixed.
5. Drop batter by teaspoonfuls onto prepared baking sheets. Bake for 12 to 15 minutes. Remove cookies and cool on a rack.

Cal 68 • Fat 1.5 g

Yield: About 4 dozen

Date Squares

These chewy bars are made with dates and cinnamon. Fresh dates can be stored in a plastic bag in the refrigerator for up to 2 weeks. Enjoy!

1 cup all-purpose flour

½ tsp. low-sodium baking powder

½ tsp. ground cinnamon

2 tbsp. maple syrup

1 cup brown sugar

6 egg whites

2 tsp. vanilla extract

2 cups chopped dates

1. Preheat oven to 300°F.
2. In a bowl, sift together flour, baking powder and cinnamon.
3. In a large bowl, combine maple syrup, brown sugar, egg whites and vanilla. Stir flour mixture into egg white mixture and mix well. Fold in dates.
4. Pour batter into an 8" square nonstick baking dish sprayed with nonstick spray.
5. Bake until done, about 30 minutes. Remove from oven, allow to cool to room temperature and cut into squares to serve.

Cal 186 • Fat 0 g

Yield: 12 Servings

201 MORE Fat•Burning RECIPES

BREADS & JAM

Raisin Bran Muffins

The molasses in these muffins provides moisture and an "old-fashioned" distinctive flavor. Chopped dates or prunes can be used instead of raisins.

2 egg whites
1 tbsp. oil
2 tbsp. applesauce
½ cup brown sugar
¼ cup molasses
1 cup flour
½ tsp. salt
½ tsp. baking soda
1½ tsp. baking powder
1 cup skim milk
1½ cups bran
½ cup raisins

1. Preheat oven to 400°F. Spray a 12-cup muffin pan with nonstick spray.
2. Beat egg whites until firm peaks form; set aside.
3. In a large bowl, combine oil, applesauce, brown sugar and molasses; beat until smooth. Sift together flour, salt, baking soda and baking powder. Add alternately with milk to molasses mixture. Add bran and raisins and stir until moistened. Fold in beaten egg whites.
4. Spoon batter into muffin cups. Bake for 15 to 20 minutes.

Cal 147 • Fat 1 g

Yield: 12 Servings

Blueberry Bran Muffins

If fresh or frozen blueberries are unavailable, raisins or dried cranberries are a tasty substitute.

1 cup natural bran
½ cup rolled oats
⅓ cup wheat germ
½ tsp. cinnamon
¼ tsp. salt
1 cup buttermilk
⅓ cup liquid honey
1 egg, lightly beaten
⅓ cup vegetable oil
½ cup all-purpose flour
1 tsp. baking powder
½ tsp. baking soda
½ cup blueberries

Topping

¼ cup packed brown sugar
¼ cup rolled oats
2 tbsp. all-purpose flour
2 tbsp. butter, melted

1. Preheat oven to 375°F. Spray a large 12-cup muffin pan with nonstick spray.
2. In a bowl, combine bran, oats, wheat germ, cinnamon and salt; stir in buttermilk and let stand for 30 minutes.
3. Add honey, egg and oil, mixing well. Stir together flour, baking powder and baking soda; add to bran mixture all at once, stirring just to moisten. Fold in blueberries.
4. Spoon batter into muffin cups, filling each about ⅔ full.
5. **Topping**: Combine sugar, oats, flour and butter. Sprinkle over muffins.
6. Bake for 20 to 25 minutes, or until firm to the touch.

Cal 185 • Fat 7.6 g

Yield: 12 Servings

Carrot-Pumpkin Muffins

Moist and packed with flavor – just imagine carrot cake with pumpkin pie!

1½ cups whole-wheat flour
1½ tsp. pumpkin pie spice
1 tsp. baking soda
½ tsp. baking powder
1 egg OR ¼ cup fat-free liquid egg substitute
1 cup canned pumpkin
¾ cup honey
2 tbsp. applesauce
1 tbsp. olive oil
1 cup shredded carrots

1. Preheat oven to 350°F. Spray a 12-cup muffin pan with nonstick spray.
2. In a large bowl, combine flour, pumpkin pie spice, baking soda and baking powder.
3. In a medium bowl, whisk egg, pumpkin, honey, applesauce and oil until smooth. Add flour mixture and stir just until combined. Do not overmix. Fold in carrots.
4. Spoon batter into muffin cups. Bake for 25 minutes, or until a toothpick inserted in the center comes out almost clean.
5. Remove muffins from pan and cool on a rack.

Cal 146 • Fat 2 g

Yield: 12 Servings

Strawberry Muffins

These strawberry muffins take less than an hour to make. Muffins can be frozen for up to 3 months. Da-Licious!!

1 cup all-purpose flour
1 cup whole-wheat flour
3 tbsp. sugar
1 tbsp. low-sodium baking powder
½ tsp. salt (optional)
½ tsp. ground nutmeg
½ tsp. ground cinnamon
2 egg whites
1 cup skim milk
¼ cup unsweetened apple sauce
1 tsp. vanilla extract
1 cup sliced fresh strawberries

1. Preheat oven to 350°F. Spray a 12-cup muffin pan with nonstick spray.
2. In a mixing bowl, combine flours, sugar, baking powder, salt, nutmeg and cinnamon. Mix well.
3. In another bowl, combine egg whites, milk, applesauce and vanilla. Stir briskly until smooth. Combine with flour mixture and stir just until all ingredients are moistened.
4. Fold in strawberries.
5. Spoon batter into muffin cups. Bake until done, about 25 minutes. Serve warm.

Cal 58 • Fat 0 g

Yield: 12 Servings

Date-Nut Bread

This date-filled bread has no added sugar or fat and not a speck of cholesterol. What it does have is 3 grams of fiber, over 10% of your needs for the day. It's also loaded with flavor!

8 oz. pkg. pitted whole dates, snipped
1 cup raisins
1½ cups boiling water
2 cups whole-wheat flour
1 tsp. baking soda
1 tsp. baking powder
¼ tsp. salt
2 slightly beaten egg whites
1 tsp. vanilla
½ cup chopped almonds

1. In a medium mixing bowl, combine dates and raisins. Pour boiling water over. Set aside to soften fruit and to cool slightly.
2. Preheat oven to 350°F. Lightly grease a 9 x 5 x 3" loaf pan; set aside.
3. In a large mixing bowl, stir together flour, baking soda, baking powder and salt. Stir egg whites and vanilla into cooled date mixture. Add date mixture and almonds to flour mixture; stir until well combined (batter will be thick).
4. Spoon batter evenly into pan. Bake 40 to 50 minutes, or until a toothpick inserted near center of loaf comes out clean.
5. Cool in pan for 10 minutes. Remove from pan; cool thoroughly on wire rack. Wrap loaf tightly with plastic wrap and store overnight before serving. Makes 1 loaf.

Cal 123 • Fat 2 g — Yield: 18 Servings

Zucchini Bread

People tell jokes about being inundated with zucchini from gardening friends – this bread is a wonderful way to enjoy low-calorie, high-fiber zucchini.

¼ cup apple juice
¼ cup skim milk
3 scant tbsp. plain nonfat yogurt
½ tsp. canola OR virgin olive oil
2 egg whites
1 cup shredded zucchini
1¼ cups whole-wheat flour
½ cup oat bran
2 tbsp. sugar
1 tbsp. baking powder
½ tsp. baking soda
1¼ tsp. ground cinnamon

1. Preheat oven to 325°F. Spray a loaf pan with nonstick spray.
2. In a medium bowl, combine apple juice, milk, yogurt, oil and egg whites; whisk to mix. Stir in zucchini.
3. In a large bowl, combine flour, oat bran, sugar, baking powder, baking soda and cinnamon.
4. Pour wet ingredients into dry ones and mix just to combine; do not overmix. Immediately transfer batter to prepared pan.
5. Bake 35 minutes, or until done.

Cal 75 • Fat 0.8 g Yield: 12 Servings

Ginger-Peach Jam

Spicy ginger helps burn fat. Ginger's stimulant properties rev your metabolism to burn fat and calories faster. Perfect with muffins and nut breads or stir a spoonful into plain, fat-free yogurt for a luscious treat.

3 lbs. peaches (about 6 cups)
3 cups granulated sugar
3 tbsp. chopped fresh ginger
2 tsp. lemon juice
¼ tsp. allspice

1. Place peaches in boiling water for 1 minute, or until skins loosen. Plunge peaches in ice water. Slip off skins, halve fruit and remove pits. Cut into 1" pieces.
2. In a large nonreactive pot, combine peaches, sugar, ginger, lemon juice and allspice. Simmer over medium heat 30 minutes, or until jam thickens and mounds on spoon
3. Ladle jam into jars and store in refrigerator for up to 2 months, or follow preserving directions in your favorite cookbook and store indefinitely.

Cal 34 • Fat 0 g

Yield: 8 Servings

CENTAX COOKBOOKS MAKE GREAT GIFTS

Flavors of Home ______ x $19.95 = $ ______
Grandma's Best ______ x $21.95 = $ ______
Grandma's Kitchen ______ x $21.95 = $ ______
Grandma's Soups & Stews with Salads, Breads & Biscuits ______ x $21.95 = $ ______
Grandma's Touch ______ x $21.95 = $ ______
201 Fat-Burning Recipes ______ x $19.95 = $ ______
201 MORE Fat-Burning Recipes ______ x $19.95 = $ ______
Create Your Own – College Survival Recipes ______ x $12.95 = $ ______
Create Your Own – Holiday Cookbook ______ x $12.95 = $ ______
Create Your Own – Recipes By Me Cookbook ______ x $12.95 = $ ______
Shipping and handling charge (total order) ______ = $ $4.00
Subtotal ______ = $ ______
In Canada add 7% GST ______ = $ ______
Total enclosed ______ = $ ______

U.S. and international orders payable in U.S. funds/Prices subject to change.

NAME: ______
STREET: ______
CITY: ______ PROV./STATE ______
COUNTRY: ______ POSTAL CODE/ZIP: ______

❒ CHEQUE ***OR*** Charge to ❒ VISA ❒ MASTERCARD

Account Number: | | | | | | | | | | | | | | | | |

Expiry Date: | | | | |

Telephone (in case we have a question about your order): ______

Make cheque or money order payable

TO: **Centax Books & Distribution**
1150 Eighth Avenue
Regina, Saskatchewan
Canada S4R 1C9

OR Order by phone, fax or email:
Phone: 1-800-667-5595
FAX: 1-800-823-6829
E-mail: centax@printwest.com

See our website for our complete range of cookbooks, gardening books, history books, etc.

www.centaxbooks.com

For fund-raising or volume purchases, contact Centax Books & Distribution for volume rates. Please allow 2-3 weeks for delivery.

CENTAX COOKBOOKS MAKE GREAT GIFTS

201 FAT-BURNING RECIPES
by Cathi Graham
Master your metabolism. Cathi Graham lost 186 pounds and has kept it off for over 10 years without dieting. This book complements her Fresh Start™ program. Although there were no foods she wouldn't allow herself, she ate a high-calorie intake of proven "fat-burning" foods. These easy recipes feature fibre-rich or high carbohydrate/low-fat foods. Calorie and fat counts are included. Here are great recipes for losing weight or just for maintaining a healthy lifestyle.
Retail $19.95 5¾" x 8½"
248 pages 5 colour photographs
ISBN 1-895292-34-4 perfect bound

GRANDMA'S KITCHEN – Comfort Cooking from Canadian Grandmas – over 200,000 sold in series
by Irene Hrechuk and Verna Zasada
Grandma's Kitchen celebrates Canadian cooking as traditional favorites from many other countries become new Canadian traditions. *Grandma's kitchen* evokes memories of delicious flavors and aromas. With this cookbook you can prepare your special childhood favorites as grandma used to make them. You can also prepare some of the fabulous recipes made by your friends' grandmas.
Retail $21.95 7" x 10"
208 pages 10 colour photographs
ISBN 1-894022-86-6 perfect bound

FLAVORS OF HOME – Creative Home Cooking
by Patti Shenfield
Back in Print! Tempting homestyle recipes feature imaginative variations to delight all cooks. Variations encourage novice cooks to be creative and offer enticing flavor variety. Basic crêpes range from sweet to savory options. A basic sourdough recipe includes cheese muffins, French loaf and other options. Soup, salad and dessert recipes all emphasize the adaptability of good basic recipes. This is creative comfort food with flavor and flair.
Retail $19.95 7" x 10"
208 pages 10 colour photographs
ISBN 1-894022-68-8 perfect bound

GRANDMA'S SOUPS & SALADS with Biscuits & Breads
by Irene Hrechuk and Verna Zasada
Over 100 superb soups and stews range from elegant chilled to hearty vegetable, seafood and meat. Over 70 fabulous salads include fruit, grains, pasta, vegetable and tossed salads. There are also over 25 satisfying yeast and quick breads. Outstanding variation suggestions effectively double the number of soup, salad and bread recipes. These are family-style recipes – grandma's comfort food.
Retail $21.95 7" x 10"
208 pages 10 colour photographs
ISBN 1-897010-02-8 perfect bound

GRANDMA'S BEST – Traditional Treats – over 200,000 sold in series
by Irene Hrechuk and Verna Zasada
Grandma's Best and *Grandma's Touch* represent the rich multicultural aspect of Canadian life and include treasured family recipes from many cultural groups. A special children's section has recipes that children love and love to make. This satisfying collection of grandma's favorite recipes will please everyone from grandkids to grandads. Here are the satisfying, comforting aromas and flavors that you remember from Grandma's kitchen.
Retail $21.95 7" x 10"
208 pages 10 colour photographs
ISBN 1-894022-66-1 perfect bound

GRANDMA'S TOUCH – A Canadian Classic – over 200,000 sold in series
by Irene Hrechuk and Verna Zasada
Enjoy your special childhood favorites as Grandma used to make them, updated for today's busy, health-conscious cooks. Enjoy your favorite comfort food from your British, Chinese, French, German, Italian, Irish, Mexican, Russian, Scandinavian and Ukrainian grandmothers. These recipes, using readily available ingredients, are economical, easy to prepare and will delight beginner and experienced cooks.
Retail $21.95 7" x 10"
208 pages 10 colour photographs
ISBN 1-895292-62-9 perfect bound

CREATE YOUR OWN COOKBOOKS

MY HOLIDAY RECIPES & TRADITIONS
ISBN 1-894022-55-6

RECIPES BY ME & OTHER SPECIAL PEOPLE
ISBN 1-894022-44-0

MY COLLEGE SURVIVAL RECIPES
ISBN 1-894022-93-9

***Create Your Own Cookbooks* each includes a roasting chart, herb and spice chart, ingredient substitutions, ingredient equivalent measures, metric conversion tables, kitchen tips and household hints.**

EACH *Create Your Own Cookbook* RETAILS FOR $12.95, 6" x 9", has 144 pages with illustrations throughout and lay-flat coil binding.